Norman Mailer was born in New Jersey in 1923. He grew up in Brooklyn and entered Harvard University when he was only sixteen. It was at university while majoring in engineering that he became interested in writing and he published his first story at the age of eighteen. During the Second World War, Mailer served in the Philippines with 112th Cavalry from Texas; those were the years that formed his internationally bestselling war novel, *The Naked and the Dead* (1948). His other books include *Barbary Shore* (1951), *The Deer Park* (1957), *Advertisements for Myself* (1959), *Deaths for the Ladies* (1962), *The Presidential Papers* (1963), *An American Dream* (1965), *Why Are We in Vietnam?* (1967), *The Armies of the Night* (1969) for which he was awarded both the Pulitzer Prize and the National Book Award, *Marilyn* (1973), and *The Fight* (1975). *The Deer Park* has been adapted into a play and successfully produced off Broadway.

In 1955 Mailer co-founded the magazine *Village Voice*, and he was the editor of *Dissent* from 1952 until 1963. For his part in demonstrations against the war in Vietnam he was gaoled in 1967.

Indisputably one of the most controversial, talented and popular authors of our time, Norman Mailer has been married four times and has six children.

Also by Norman Mailer

The Naked and the Dead
Barbary Shore
The Deer Park
Advertisements for Myself
Death for the Ladies (and other Disasters)
The Presidential Papers
An American Dream
Why Are We in Vietnam?
The Armies of the Night
Miami and the Siege of Chicago
Of a Fire on the Moon
The Prisoner of Sex
Maidstone
Existential Errands
Marilyn
The Faith of Graffiti
The Fight

Norman Mailer

Cannibals and Christians

PANTHER
GRANADA PUBLISHING
London Toronto Sydney New York

Abridged edition published by Granada Publishing Limited
in Panther Books 1979

ISBN 0 586 04851 0

Complete edition first published in Great Britain by
André Deutsch Ltd 1967
Copyright © Norman Mailer 1966

Granada Publishing Limited
Frogmore, St Albans, Herts AL2 2NF
and
3 Upper James Street, London W1R 4BP
1221 Avenue of the Americas, New York, NY 10020, USA
117 York Street, Sydney, NSW 2000, Australia
100 Skyway Avenue, Toronto, Ontario, Canada M9W 3A6
110 Northpark Centre, 2193 Johannesburg, South Africa
CML Centre, Queen & Wyndham, Auckland 1, New Zealand

Set, printed and bound in Great Britain by
Cox & Wyman Ltd, Reading
Set in Intertype Times

Granada ®
Granada Publishing ®

to Lyndon B. Johnson
whose name inspired young men to cheer for me in public

Contents

Acknowledgment

Acknowledgment is made to the following magazines and publishers in whose pages these essays first appeared.

Dissent: for 'Introducing Our Argument'.

Esquire: for 'In the Red Light: A History of the Republican Convention in 1964', 'Some Children of the Goddess', and 'The Last Night'.

Evergreen Review: for 'The Killer'.

Paris Review: for 'The Art of Fiction' originally published in a somewhat different form.

Playboy: portions of 'Petty Notes on Some Sex in America' appeared originally in PLAYBOY Magazine, © 1961, 1962 by HMH Publishing Co.

The Viking Press, Inc.: for 'The Art of Fiction' published in its original form in WRITERS AT WORK, III, 1967.

Publisher's Note

This book is a collection of writings from 1960 to 1966. The collection was originally published in hardback in an extended form.

To link the pieces, Norman Mailer wrote a continuing presentation – titled an *Argument* – which runs along in italics. He explained, in his original introduction, 'Argument is a curious word; it has odd attachments to the past – I would not certify its flavour to be necessarily eighteenth century, or scholastic, or 180 AD, but since we deal here often with America, with all us electronic descendants of Rome, let the word give a taste of the Latin. Even if it does not, nothing is more acceptable to America than an excess of baroque. So: *Cannibals and Christians*, a book with an Argument.'

PART ONE: LAMBS

Introducing Our Argument

In Provincetown, a friend brought a gift. She brought a big round metal GULF *sign seven feet in diameter which another friend had discovered in the town dump and rescued. The hair of fashion came alert: we might make a coffee table. While we drank, we could look at the shading in the orange and blue letters. Poets in the room could contemplate the value of –* GULF *– even as a novitiate in Yoga will fix on the resonance of* OM. *Musicians could explore the tick of the cocktail glass against the metal. Intellectuals could . . .*

What a deal intellectuals could do. There would be those to claim Pop art is the line where culture meets mass civilization, and so Pop art is the vehicle for bringing taste to the masses; others to argue the debauch of Capitalism has come to the point where it crosses the doorstep and inhabits the place where you set your drink. And those to say fun; *fun is the salvation of society.*

It would go on: some might decide that putting a huge gasoline company's totem into one's private space helped to mock civilization and its hired man, the corporation; others would be certain the final victory of the corporation was near when we felt affection for the device by which a corporation advertised itself.

At last, nothing was done with the sign. I did not want to go through dialogue and the same dialogue about why it was there and whether it was good it was there, or bad it was there, and in truth I did not want the work of disposing of it when the fashion had passed. So I left the sign to rust on the beach, a mile from its burial ground on the dump.

List the symptoms. We live in a time which has created the art of the absurd. It is our art. It contains happenings, Pop art, camp, a theater of the absurd, a homosexual genius

*who spent thirty years as a thief; black humor is its wit; the
dances are livid and solitary – they are also orgiastic: orgy
or masturbation? – the first question posed by the art of the
absurd. So the second: is the art rational or absurd? Do we
have the art because the absurd is the patina of waste, and
we are waiting in the pot for the big roar of waters when the
world goes down the pipe? Or are we face to face with a
desperate but most rational effort from the deepest re-
sources of the unconscious of us all to rescue civilization
from the pit and plague of its bedding, that gutted swinish
foul old bedding on which two centuries of imperialism,
high finance, moral hypocrisy and horror have lain. The
skulls of black men and the bowels of the yellow race are in
that bed, the death of the Bride of the Sabbath is in that bed
with the ashes of the concentration camp and the ashes of
the Kabbala, moonshots fly like flares across black dreams,
and the Beatles – demons or saints? – give shape to a haircut
which looks from the rear like nothing so much as an atomic
cloud. Apocalypse or debauch is upon us. And we are close
to dead. There are faces and bodies like gorged maggots on
the dance floor, on the highway, in the city, in the stadium;
they are a host of chemical machines who swallow the pro-
duct of chemical factories, aspirin, preservatives, stimulant,
relaxant, and breathe out their chemical wastes into a pol-
luted air. The sense of a long last night over civilization is
back again; it has perhaps not been here so intensely in
thirty years, not since the Nazis were prospering, but it is
coming back.*

*Well, it has been the continuing obsession of this writer
that the world is entering a time of plague. And the con-
tinuing metaphor for the obsession – a most disagreeable
metaphor – has been cancer. The argument is old by now: its
first assumption is that cancer is a disease different from
other diseases, an ultimate disease against which all other
diseases are in design to protect us.*

*The difficulty – for one can always convince the literary
world to accept a metaphor if one remains loyal to it – is*

that my obsession is not merely an obsession, I fear, but insight into the nature of things, perhaps the deepest insight I have, and this said with no innocence of the knowledge that the plague can have its home within, and these condemnations come to no more than the grapplings of a man with a curse on his flesh, or even the probability that society partakes of the plague and its critic partakes, and each wars against the other, the man and the society each grappling with his own piece of the plague, as if, indeed, we are each of us born not only with our life but with our death, with our variety of death, good death and bad, and it is the act of each separate man to look to free himself from that part of his existence which was born with the plague. Some succeed, some fail, and some of us succeed nobly for we clear our own plague and help to clear the plague upon the world, and others succeed, others – are we those? – you don't know – who clear their plague by visiting it upon friends, passing their disease into the flesh and mind of near bodies, and into the circuits of the world. And they poison the wells and get away free, some of them – they get away free if there is a devil and he has power, and that is something else we do not know. But the plague remains, that mysterious force which erects huge, ugly, and aesthetically emaciated buildings as the world ostensibly grows richer, and proliferates new diseases as medicine presumably grows wiser, nonspecific diseases, families of viruses, with new names and no particular location. And products deteriorate in workmanship as corporations improve their advertising, wars shift from carnage and patriotism to carnage and surrealism, sex shifts from whiskey to drugs. And all the food is poisoned. And the waters of the sea we are told. And there is always the sound of some electric motor in the ear.

In a modern world which produces mediocrities at an accelerating rate, and keeps them alive by surgical gymnastics which go beyond anyone's patience but the victim, the doctor, and the people who expect soon to be on the operating tables themselves; in a civilization where compassion

*is of political use and is stratified in welfare programs which
do not build a better society but shore up a worse; in a world
whose ultimate logic is war, because in a world of war all
overproduction and overpopulation is possible since
peoples and commodities may be destroyed wholesale – in a
breath, a world of such hypercivilization is a world not of
adventurers, entrepreneurs, settlers, social arbiters, pro-
letarians, agriculturists, and other egocentric types of a dy-
namic society, but is instead a world of whirlpools and
formlessness where two huge types begin to reemerge, types
there at the beginning of it all: Cannibals and Christians.*

*We are martyrs all these days. All that Right Wing which
believes there is too much on earth and too much of it is
second-rate, all of that Right Wing which runs from staunch
Republicanism to the extreme Right Wing, and then half
around the world through the ghosts of the Nazis, all of that
persecuted Right Wing which sees itself as martyr, knows
that it knows how to save the world: one can save the world
by killing off what is second-rate. So they are the Cannibals
– they believe that survival and health of the species comes
from consuming one's own, not one's near-own, but one's
own species. So the pure cannibal has only one taboo on
food – he will not eat the meat of his own family. Other men
he will of course consume. Their virtues he will conserve in
his own flesh, their vices he will excrete, but to kill and to
eliminate is his sense of human continuation.*

*Then come our Christians. They are the commercial. The
commercial is the invention of a profoundly Christian
nation – it proceeds to sell something in which it does not
altogether believe, and it interrupts the mood. We are all of
us Christians: Jews, liberals, Bolsheviks, anarchists, Social-
ists, Communists, Keynesians, Democrats, Civil Righters,
beatniks, ministers, moderate Republicans, pacifists. Teach-
inners, doctors, scientists, professors, Latin Americans, new
African nations, Common Marketers, even Mao Tse-tung.
Doubtless. From Lyndon Johnson to Mao Tse-tung, we are
all Christians. We believe man is good if given a chance, we*

*believe man is open to discussion, we believe science is the
salvation of ill, we believe death is the end of discussion;
ergo we believe nothing is so worthwhile as human life. We
think no one should go hungry. So forth. What characterizes
Christians is that most of them are not Christian and have no
interest left in Christ. What characterizes the Cannibals is
that most of them are born Christian, think of Jesus as Love,
and get an erection from the thought of whippings, blood,
burning crosses, burning bodies, and screams in mass graves.
Whereas their counterpart, the Christians – the ones who are
not Christian but whom we choose to call Christian – are
utterly opposed to the destruction of human life and succeed
within themselves in starting all the wars of our own time,
since every war since the Second World War has been
initiated by liberals or Communists; these Christians also
succeed by their faith in science to poison the nourishment
we eat and the waters of the sea, to alter the genetics of our
beasts, and to break the food chains of nature.*

*Yet every year the girls are more beautiful, the athletes
are better. So the dilemma remains. Is the curse on the world
or on oneself? Does the world get better, no matter how,
getting better and worse as part of the same process, or does
the world get better in spite of the fact it is getting worse,
and we are approaching the time when an apocalypse will
pass through the night? We live after all in a time which
interrupts the mood of everything alive.*

*I would submit that everything here has been written in the
years of the plague, and so I must see myself sometimes as
physician more than rifleman, a physician half blind, not so
far from drunk, his nerve to be recommended not at every
occasion, nor his hand to hold at each last bed, but a noble
physician nonetheless, noble at least in his ideal, for he is
certain that there is a strange disease before him, an un-
known illness, a phenomenon which partakes of mystery,
nausea, and honor; if the nausea gives him pause and the
honor fear, still the mystery summons, he is a physician,
he must try to explore the mystery. So, he does, and by*

different methods too many a time. We will not go on to speak of the medicines and the treatment, of surgeon, bonesetter, lab analyst – no, the metaphor has come to the end of its way. These writings are then attempts to deal with mysteries which offer the presumption that there is an answer to be found, or a clue. So I proceed, even as a writer when everything goes well, and perhaps a few matters are uncovered and more I know are left to chase. What follows, at any rate, are some explorations of the theme stated here, some talk of Cannibals and Christians, some writings on politics, on literary matters, on philosophy – save us all – on philosophy.

IN THE RED LIGHT: *A History of the Republican Convention in 1964*

. . . He had drawn the burning city, a great bonfire of architectural styles, ranging from Egyptian to Cape Cod colonial. Through the center, winding from left to right, was a long hill street and down it, spilling into the middle foreground, came the mob carrying baseball bats and torches. For the faces of its members, he was using the innumerable sketches he had made of the people who come to California to die; the cultists of all sorts, economic as well as religious, the wave, airplane, funeral and preview watchers – all those poor devils who can only be stirred by the promise of miracles and then only to violence. A super 'Dr Know-All Pierce-All' had made the necessary promise of miracles and they were marching behind his banner in a great united front of screwballs and screwboxes to purify the land. No longer bored, they sang and danced joyously in the red light of the flames.

      – NATHANAEL WEST, *The Day of the Locust*

Now, the city was beautiful, it was still the most beautiful city in the United States, but like all American cities it was a

casualty of the undeclared war. There had been an undis-
closed full-scale struggle going on in America for twenty
years – it was whether the country would go mad or not.
And the battle line of that war (which showed that yes
slowly the country was losing the war, we were indeed going
mad) was of course the progress of the new roads, buildings,
and supermarkets which popped out all over the cities of the
nation. San Francisco was losing her beauty. Monstrous cor-
porations in combine with monstrous realtors had erected
monstrous boxes of Kleenex ten, twenty, thirty stories high
through the downtown section, and the new view from Tele-
graph Hill had shards of glass the size of a mountain wall
stuck into the soft Italian landscape of St Francis' City. The
San Francisco Hilton, for an example, while close to twenty
stories high was near to a square block in size and looked
from the street to have the proportions and form of a cube
of sugar. It was a dirty sugar-white in color and its windows
were set in an odd elongated checkerboard, a harlequin pat-
tern in which each window was offset from the one above
and beneath like the vents in a portable radio.

The Hilton was only six weeks old, but already it was one
of the architectural wonders of the world, for its insides were
composed in large part of an automobile ramp on which it
was possible to drive all the way up to the eleventh floor,
open a door and lo! you were in your hotel corridor, twenty
feet from your own room door. It was a startling way to
exhaust the internal space of a hotel, but it had one huge
American advantage: any guest at the Hilton could drive all
the way to his room without ever having to steer a lady
through the lobby. Of course, after all those automobile
ramps, there was not much volume left, so the rooms were
small, the rooms were very small for seventeen dollars a day,
and the windows were placed to the extreme left or right of
the wall and ran from ceiling to floor, in order to allow the
building to appear to the outside eye like a radio being car-
ried by a model who worked in the high nude. The carpets
and wallpapers, the drapes and the table tops were plastic,

the bathroom had the odor of burning insecticide. It developed that the plastic cement used to finish the tiling gave off this odor during the months it took to dry. Molecules were being tortured everywhere.

Well, that was American capitalism gainfully employed. It had won the war. It had won it in so many places you could picture your accommodations before you arrived. Such is the nature of the promiscuous. Flying out, way out on the jet, on the way West, not yet at the Hilton but knowing it would be there, I got into a conversation with the man who sat at the window, an Australian journalist named Moffitt, a short fellow with a bushwacker's mustache; and he scolded me for reading Buchanan's book, *Who Killed Kennedy?* He wanted to know why a man of my intelligence bothered with trash. Well, the country had never been the same since Kennedy was assassinated, courtesy was ready to reply; some process of derailment, begun with Hemingway's death and the death of Marilyn Monroe, had been racing on now through the months, through the heavens, faster than the contrails of our jet across the late afternoon mind of America; so one looked for clues where they could be found. It would be easier to know that Oswald had done it all by himself, or as an accomplice to ten other men, or was innocent, or twice damned; anything was superior to that sense of the ship of state battering its way down swells of sea, while in the hold cargo was loose and ready to slide.

This conversation did not of course take place – an Astrojet is not the vehicle for metaphorical transactions, it is after all still another of the extermination chambers of the century – slowly the breath gives up some microcosmic portion of itself, green plastic and silver-gray plastic, the nostrils breathe no odor of materials which existed once as elements of nature, no wood, no stone, no ore, time molders like a sponge in the sink. But Moffitt was Australian and fascinated with America, and had his quick comments to make, some provincial, some pure shrewd; finally he poked his finger on something I had never put together for myself, not quite: 'Why is it,' he asked, 'that all the new stuff you build here, including the interior furnishings of this airplane, looks like a child's nursery?'

And that is what it was. The inside of our airplane was like a child's plastic nursery, a dayroom in the children's ward, and if I had been Quentin Compson, I might have answered, 'Because we want to go back, because the nerves grew in all the wrong ways. Because we developed habits which are suffocating us to death. I tell you, man, we do it because we're sick, we're a sick nation, we're sick to the edge of vomit and so we build our lives with materials which smell like vomit, polyethylene and bakelite and fiberglass and styrene. Yes, our schools look like nurseries, and our factories and our temples, our kitchens and our johns, our airports and our libraries and our offices, we are one great big bloody nursery attached to a doctor's waiting room, and we are sick, we're very sick, maybe we always were sick, maybe the Puritans carried the virus and were so odious the British were right to drive them out, maybe we're a nation of culls and weeds and half-crazy from the start.'

Nobody of course was Quentin Compson, nobody spoke that way any more, but the question was posed by a ghost and so had to linger: was there indeed a death in the seed which brought us here? Was the country extraordinary or accursed, a junkyard where even the minnows gave caviar in the filthy pond in the fierce electric American night?

I

I must see the things; I must see the men.

Burke, *Reflections on the Revolution in France*

At the Mark Hopkins on Saturday morning two days before the convention would begin, the atmosphere had the same agreeable clean rather healthy excitement (that particular American excitement) one picks up on the morning

of a big football game. The kids were out, the children who
were for Goldwater and those who were for Scranton, and
they milled about in the small open courtyard of the hotel,
and in the small hopelessly congested lobby where lines one
hundred long were waiting for each of the three overworked
elevators beating up to the twelfth and fourteenth floors,
Scranton and Goldwater Headquarters respectively. It was a
clear day outside, one of those cool sunny days in July when
San Francisco is as nice as New York on a beautiful day in
October, and the city fell away from Nob Hill in a perfect
throw. There were apples in the air. It was a perfect football
day. There was even wistfulness to be eighteen and have a
date for lunch before the game. So the teams lined up first
this way in one's mind, the children, adolescents, and young
men and women for Goldwater to one side, the Scrantons to
the other, and you could tell a lot about the colleges and the
teams by looking at the faces. The Goldwater girls and boys
were for the most part innocent, and they tended to have
large slightly protruded jaws, not unlike Big Barry himself,
and blue eyes – an astonishing number had blue eyes (was
the world finally coming to the war of the blue-eyed versus
the brown-eyed?) – and they were simple, they were small-
town, they were hicky, the boys tended to have a little acne,
an introspective pimple or two by the corner of the mouth
or the side of the chin, a lot of the boys looked solemn and
serious, dedicated but slightly blank – they could fix a tran-
sistor radio, but a word like 'Renaissance' would lay a soft
wound of silence, stupefaction in their brain. They were
idealists, nearly every last one of them, but they did not
speak of the happier varieties of idealism; one thought of
Lutherans from North Dakota, 4-H from Minnesota, and
Eagle Scouts from Maine. Many of them wore eyeglasses.
They were thrifty young men, hardworking young men,
polite, slightly paralyzed before the variety of life, but ready
to die for a cause. It was obvious they thought Goldwater
was one of the finest men ever to be born into American life.
And they were stingy, they wore store-bought ready-mades,

skinny kids in twenty-dollar suits and that pinch of the jaw, that recidivism of the gums which speaks of false teeth before you are fifty.

The Goldwater girls ran to two varieties. There were the models who had been hired for the purpose, and they were attractive but not very imaginative, they looked like hookers on horses, and then there were the true followers, the daughters of delegates, the California children who belonged to one Goldwater club or another. They were younger than the models of course, they were most of them fifteen, sixteen, not even seventeen, wearing cowboy hats and white vests and shirts with fringes, white riding boots; nearly all of them were blond and they had simple rather sweet faces, the sort of faces which television commercials used to use for such product fodder as biscuit batter before the commercials turned witty; these Goldwater girls had the faces of young ladies who listened to their parents, particularly to their fathers, they were full of character, but it was the character of tidiness, industry, subservience – unlike the Goldwater boys who looked on the whole not unintelligent though slightly maniacal in the singularity of their vision (the way young physicists look slightly maniacal) the girls seemed to be just about all quite dumb. There was one blond little girl who was lovely, pretty enough to be a starlet, but she left a pang because her eyes when open were irremediably dim. Taken altogether, boys and girls, they were like the graduating class of a high school in Nebraska. The valedictorian would write his speech on the following theme: Why is the United States the Greatest Nation on Earth?

Whereas the kids who were for Scranton were prep-school or countryday. Some of the boys were plump and merry, some were mildly executive, but they shared in common that slightly complacent air of success which is the only curse of the fraternity president or leader of the student council. They were keen, they tended to be smooth, they had a penchant for bow ties and they were the kind to drive Triumphs or Pontiac convertibles, while the Goldwater boys would be

borrowing their father's Dodge Dart (except for the one in a
hundred who was automotive in his genius and so had built
a dragster to top out at one-six-five). Then there were the
Scranton boys who were still the descendants of Holden
Caulfield. Faces like theirs had been seen for Stevenson in
'60 in L.A. against J.F.K., and faces like theirs might appear
(one would hope) in '68 for still another, but for now they
were for the nearest candidate with wit, class, and the born
foreknowledge of defeat. Slim, slightly mournful, certainly
acerb, and dubious of the fraternity presidents with whom
they had made cause, the Holden Caulfields were out for
Scranton, and looked a size overmatched by the girls who
were for Scranton, good-looking most of them, slightly
spoiled, saucy, full of peeves, junior debs doing their best to
be cool and so wearing their hair long with a part down the
center in such a way that the face, sexy, stripped of makeup
(except for some sort of white libidinous wax on the lips)
was half-concealed by a Gothic arch of falling tresses. Such
were Scranton's parts, such were Goldwater's, as the chil-
dren shaped up for the game.

*In this state of ... warfare between the noble ancient landed
interest and the new monied interest, the ... monied interest is
in its nature more ready for any adventure; and its possessors
more disposed to new enterprises of any kind. Being of a recent
acquisition, it falls in more naturally with any novelties. It is
therefore the kind of wealth which will be resorted to by all
who wish for change.*

— Burke, *Reflections on the Revolution in France*

*Among the young industrial and financial monopolies of the
West and Southwest that want a 'bigger slice of the capitalist
profit pie', Mr Vasilyev listed H. L. Hunt, the Texas multi-
millionaire, the Lockheed Aircraft Corporation, the Douglas
Aircraft Company, the Boeing Company and the Northrup
Corporation and the Giannini 'financial empire' headed by the
Bank of America.*

*These are the forces, Mr Vasilyev said, that overcame the
last-minute effort by 'Wall Street, the Boston financial group
and the Pennsylvania industrial complex' to promote the can-
didacy of Governor William W. Scranton of Pennsylvania at
the Republican convention last month.*

*'But the "new money" of the West proved to be stronger than
the old money of the Northeast,' the Soviet commentator said.*

— *New York Times*, August 13, 1964

For a time it had been interesting history. You will remem-
ber that Scranton decided to run for nomination after a talk
in Gettysburg on June 6 with President Eisenhower. He left
with the solid assumption he would receive Eisenhower's
support, solid enough for Governor Scranton's public-
relations machine to announce this fact to the nation. That
night or early next morning President Eisenhower received a
phone call from George Humphrey. Eisenhower had been
planning to visit Humphrey in Cleveland during the week of
the Governor's Conference. But it developed Barry Gold-
water had already been invited to be at Humphrey's home as
well. A social difficulty thus presented itself. Humphrey re-
solved it in this fashion: Eisenhower would understand if,
under the circumstances, Goldwater having been invited
first . . .

Ike knew what that meant. If his old friend, crony, sub-
ordinate and private brain trust George Humphrey was wil-
ling to let the old gander-in-chief come out second on a
collision of invitations, then Ike had picked a loser, Ike was
in danger of being a loser himself. Well, Ike hadn't come out
of Abilene, Kansas, all those years ago *ever* to end on the
losing side. So he waddled back to the middle. He phoned
Bill Scranton you will remember but an hour before Scran-
ton was ready to announce his candidacy at the Governor's
Conference on June 7, and told Scranton he could not be
party to a 'cabal'. It was obvious to everybody in America
that the old man had not labored through the night and
through the day to make the truth of his first conversation

with the young man stand out loud and clear in the high sun of ten a.m.

Still, one could not feel too sorry for the young man. It is never easy to grieve for a candidate of the Establishment, particularly the Republican Establishment of the East, which runs a spectrum from the Duke of Windsor to Jerome Zerbe, from Thomas E. Dewey to Lowell Thomas, from Drue Heinz to Tex and Jinx, from Maine to Nassau, New York to South of France, from Allen Dulles to Henry Luce, Igor Cassini to Joe Alsop, from Sullivan & Cromwell to Cartier's, and from Arthur Krock to Tuxedo Park.

Well, the last two years, all the way from Arthur Krock to Tuxedo Park, you could hear that Bill Scranton was going to be the Republican candidate in '64. Attempts might be made to argue: Goldwater looks strong, somebody could say at a dinner table; hasn't got a chance, the Establishment would give back – it's going to be Scranton. What was most impressive is that the Establishment did not bother to photograph their man, immerse him in publicity, or seek to etch his image. It was taken for granted that when the time came, doors would open, doors would shut, figures would be inserted, heads would be removed, a whiff of incense, a whisk of wickedness – Scranton would be the candidate.

Of course, Goldwater, or the Goldwater organization or *some* organization, kept picking up delegates for Goldwater, and from a year away there was a bit of sentiment that it might be easier to make a deal with Goldwater, it might be easier to *moderate* him than to excise him. Once upon a time, J. P. Morgan would doubtless have sent some bright young man out on the Southern Pacific with a bag full of hundred-dollar bills. Now, however, possessing a mass media, the buy-off could take place in public. Last November, three weeks before J.F.K. was assassinated, *Life* Magazine put Goldwater on their cover wearing a pearl-gray Stetson and clean, pressed, faded blue work shirt and Levi's while his companion, a Palomino named Sunny, stood with one of the Senator's hands on his bridle, the other laid over the vein of his nose. It was Hopalong Cassidy all baby fat removed, it gave promise of the campaign to come: the image of Kennedy was now to be combated by Sheriff B. Morris Goldwater, the Silver Gun of the West. It was one of those pictures worth ten thousand speeches it gave promise of delivering a million votes. It was also a way of stating that the Establishment was not yet unalterably opposed to Goldwater, and could yet help him, as it had with this cover. But inside the magazine across the heads of seven million readers, another message was delivered to the Senator.

Financial interests in Ohio, Illinois, Texas, Los Angeles and San Francisco – all centers of wealth independent of eastern ties – have been lining up money and intense local pressure for Goldwater. But ... people fail to realize there's a difference in kinds of money ... Old money has political power but new money has only purchasing power ... When you get to a convention, you don't buy delegates. But you do put the pressure on people who control the delegates – the people who owe the old money for their stake.

Which was a way to remind Goldwater there were concessions to make. It was in foreign affairs that Goldwater had the most to explain about his policies.

Barry Goldwater (went Life's *conclusion) represents a valuable impulse in the American politics of '64. He does not yet clearly represent all that a serious contender for the Presidency should. 'Guts without depth' and 'a man of one-sentence solutions' are the epithets of his critics. The time has come for him to rebut them if he can.*

Two months later Goldwater announced his formal candidacy for the Republican nomination, and issued a pamphlet called 'Senator Goldwater Speaks Out on the Issues'.

Written in that milk-of-magnesia style which is charac-
teristic of such tracts, one could no longer be certain what he
thought – he had moved from being a man of 'one-sentence
solutions' to a man who showed a preference for many im-
precise sentences. Barry was treading water. As he did, his
people, his organization, kept picking up delegates. It was
not until he voted against the Civil Rights Bill that the open
battle between old money and new was at last engaged. Too
late on the side of the East. To anyone who knew a bit about
the workings of the Establishment, a mystery was present.
For unless the Establishment had become most suddenly
inept, there was a buried motive in the delay, a fear, as if the
Eastern money were afraid of some force in the American
mind racing to power in defiance of them, some mystique
from out the pure accelerating delirium of a crusade which
would make cinder of the opposition. So they had waited, all
candidates but Rockefeller had waited, none willing to draw
the fires of the Right until Scranton was flushed by the ebb
and flow, the mystery or murmur, in an old man's throat.

Somewhat later that morning, one saw Scranton in a press
conference at the San Francisco Hilton. The Corinthian
Room on the ballroom floor (Press Headquarters) was a
white room, perhaps forty-five feet by forty feet with a low
ceiling and a huge puff of a modern chandelier made up of
pieces of plastic which looked like orange candy. The carpet
was an electric plastic green, the bridge seats (some two hun-
dred of them) were covered in a plastic the color of wet
aspirin, and the walls were white, a hospital-sink white. The
practical effect was to leave you feeling like a cold cut set in
the white tray of a refrigerator.

The speaker, however, was like a fly annealed on the elec-
tric-light bulb of the refrigerator. The banks of lights were
turned on him, movie lights, TV lights, four thousand watts
in the eye must be the average price a politician pays for his
press conference. It gives them all a high instant patina, their
skin responding to the call of the wild; there is danger, be-
cause the press conference creates the moment when the

actor must walk into the gears of the machine. While it is a hundred-to-one or a thousand-to-one he will make no mistake, his career can be extinguished by a blunder. Unless one is making news on a given day – which is to say an important announcement is to be made – the press conference is thus a virtuoso price to be paid for remaining in the game, since there are all too many days when it is to the interest of the speaker, or of his party, or his wing of the party, to make no particular news, but rather to repress news. Still the speaker must not be too dull, or he will hurt his own position, his remarks will be printed too far back in the paper. So he must be interesting without being revealing. Whereas it is to the interest of the press to make him revealing. A delicate game of balance therefore goes on. Nixon used to play well until the day of his breakdown. Eisenhower was once good at it. Goldwater was considered bad at this game, sufficiently bad that at the convention he held but one press conference before his nomination, and in the six preceding weeks had given but two.

An opportunity to observe the game in operation came with Melvin Laird who tried to convince the Press Corps that the Republican platform was liberal, strong on civil rights, critical of extremists, and yet true to Goldwater. Laird, a smooth vigorous man with a bald domelike head, held the breech for half an hour, ducking questions with grace the way Negroes used once to duck baseballs in a carnival. When he got into trouble (it was after all a most untenable position), he called on one of the most necessary rules of the game, which is that you don't insult the good character of the speaker. So Laird would finally say, 'We worked hard on this platform, it's a good platform, I'm proud of it.' That made the questioners retreat and regroup for a new attack.

Now Scranton's press conferences were of course different – because no one could be certain if Scranton was part of the game or a wild hare diverting the chase from every true scent. The result was a choppiness to the questioning, a sense of irritation, a hint of vast contempt from the Press Corps; a reporter despises a politician who is not professional, for the game then becomes surrealistic, and it is the function of games to keep dreams, dread and surrealism out in the night where they belong. They would dog at Scranton, they would try to close: *Governor, Governor, could you give the name of any delegate who has moved over from Goldwater to you?* No, we are not prepared to say at this time, would come the answer. *Are there any?* (Titter from the audience.) Certainly. *But you do not care to say?* Not at this time. *Governor* (a new man now), *is there any truth to the rumor you are going to concede before the convention begins?* None whatsoever. *Governor, is it not true that you may be willing to run for vice-president?* For the eighty-eighth time, it is certainly not true. *Unqualifiedly?* Yes (said Scranton sadly) unqualifiedly.

He stood there like a saint, a most curious kind of saint. If he had been an actor he would have played the Dauphin to Ingrid Bergman's Joan of Arc. He was obviously, on superficial study, a weak and stubborn man. One felt he had been spoiled when he was young by a lack of testing. It was not that he lacked bravery, it was that he had lacked all opportunity to be brave for much too long, and now he was not so much engaged in a serious political struggle as in a puberty rite. It was incredible that this pleasant urbane man, so self-satisfied, so civilized, so reasonable, so innocent of butchers' tubs and spleens and guts (that knowledge which radiates with full ceremony off Khrushchev's halo), should be now in fact the man the Eastern Establishment had picked as their candidate for President. He had a fatal flaw to his style, he was just very slightly delicate the way, let us say, a young Madison Avenue executive will seem petulant next to the surly vigor of a president of a steel corporation. Scranton had none of the heft of a political jockstrapper like Goldwater; no, rather he had the big wide thin-lipped mouth of a clown – hopeless! If the roles had been reversed, if it had been Scranton with six hundred delegates and Gold-

water who led a rush in the last four weeks to steal the land,
why Goldwater might still have won. Scranton was decent
but some part of his soul seemed to live in the void. Doubt-
less he had been more formidable when he began, but he had
been losing for four weeks, one loss after another, delegates,
delegations, caucuses, he had been losing with Eisenhower,
he had lost with Dirksen, he had lost Illinois, he was losing
Ohio, his wheeler-dealers stood by idle wheels; you cannot
deal when you are losing delegates, there is nothing to offer
the delegate but the salvation of his soul, and the delegate
has put salvation in hock a long time ago. So Scranton had
begun with the most resistant of missions – there are few
works in life so difficult as to pry delegates loose from a man
who has a nomination virtually won. To be a delegate and
stick with the loser is a kind of life, but no delegate can face
the possibility of going from a winner to a loser; the losses
are not measurable. People are in politics to win. In these
circumstances, consider the political weight lifting required
of Scranton. He announces his candidacy four weeks before
the convention, Goldwater within fifty votes of the nomi-
nation. Is Scranton to pull delegates loose from such a scene
by an unhappy faculty for getting pictures taken with his
legs in the air doing polkas, R.C.A.F. exercises, and back-
hands in tennis? One knows Scranton's the product of a
good many evenings when Eastern gentry circled around
cigars and brandy and decided on poor Bill because he was
finally not offensive to any. But it would have taken Paul
Bunyan to claw into Goldwater's strength from four weeks
out. His two hundred plus of Southern delegates were firm
as marble, firm as their hatred of Civil Rights. And there
was much other strength for Barry from the Midwest and
the West, a hard core of delegates filled with hot scalding
hatred for the Eastern Establishment. They were (unlike
the children who were for Goldwater), this hard core of del-
egates, composed in large part of the kind of tourists who
had been poisoning the air of hotel lobbies for twenty years.
You could see them now with their Goldwater buttons,

ensconced in every lobby, a Wasp Mafia where the grapes of wrath were stored. Not for nothing did the White Anglo-Saxon Protestant have a five-year subscription to *Reader's Digest* and *National Geographic*, high colonics and arthritis, silver-rimmed spectacles, punched-out bellies, and that air of controlled schizophrenia which is the merit badge for having spent one's life on Main Street. Indeed there was general agreement that the basic war was between Main Street and Wall Street. What was not seen so completely is that this war is the Wagnerian drama of the Wasp. For a century now the best of the White Protestants have been going from the farm to the town, leaving the small city for the larger one, transferring from Shaker Heights High to Lawrenceville, from Missouri State Teacher's to Smith, from Roast Turkey to Cordon Rouge, off rectitude onto wickedness, out of monogamy into *Les Liaisons Dangereuses*, from *Jane Eyre* to *Candy*; it's a long trip from the American Legion's Annual Ball to the bust-outs of Southampton. There's the unheard cry of a wounded coyote in all the minor leagues of the Junior League, in all the tacky doings of each small town, the grinding rasp of envy rubs the liver of each big frog in his small pond, no hatred like hatred for the East in the hearts of those who were left behind: the horror in the heart of social life in America is that one never knows whether one is snubbed for too much or too little, whether one was too fine or not fine enough, too graceless or too possessed of special grace, too hungry for power or not ambitious enough – the questions are burning and never answered because the Establishment of the East rarely rejects, it merely yields or ignores, it promises and forgets, it offers to attend your daughter's party and somehow does not quite show up, or comes that fraction too late which is designed to spoil the high anticipation of the night. (Or worse, leaves a fraction too early.) The Wasps who were for Goldwater were the social culls of that Eastern Society which ran the land, yes, the Goldwater Wasps were the old doctors of Pasadena with their millions in stock and their grip on the A.M.A., the small-town newspaper editors, the president of the second most important bank, the wives of Texas oil, yes the wives and family of all the prominent and prosperous who had a fatal touch of the hick, all the Western ladies who did the Merengue at El Morocco on a trip to New York, and did it not quite well enough, you could just hear the giggles in the throat of Archie or Lightning Dick or Sad One-Eye, the Haitian and/or Jamaican who had taught them how. Yes the memory of those social failures is the saliva of intellectual violence. The old Goldwater Wasps, the ones who had been sitting in the hotel lobbies, had an insane sting to their ideas – they were for birching America's bare bottom where Come-you-nisms collected: white and Negro equality; sexual excess; Jew ideas; dirty linen, muddled thinking, lack of respect for the Constitution. The Right in America had an impacted consistency of constipation to their metaphor. Small wonder they dreamed of a Republican purge. The Wasps were full of psychic wastes they could not quit – they had moved into the Middle West and settled the West, they had won the country, and now they were losing it to the immigrants who had come after and the descendants of slaves. They had watched as their culture was adulterated, transported, converted into some surrealist mélange of public piety *cum* rock and roll, product of the movies and television, of the mass media where sons of immigrants were so often king, yes the Wasps did not understand what was going on, they were not so ready after all to listen to those of their ministers who would argue that America had a heritage of sin and greed vis-à-vis the Negro, and those sins of the blood must be paid; they were not at all ready to listen to the argument that America's industry had been built out of the hardworking hard-used flesh of five generations of immigrants, no, they were Christian but they did not want to hear any more about the rights of others, they suffered from the private fear they were not as good, not as tough, not as brave as their great-grandfathers, they suffered from the intolerable fear that they were not nearly so good nor so tough as those other Christians close to two thousand years ago who faced Romans, so they were now afraid of the East which had dominated the fashion and style of their life, they were ready to murder the East, the promiscuous adulterous East – in a good fast nuclear war they might allow the Russians a fair crack at New York – yes they were loaded with one hatred: the Eastern Establishment was not going to win again, this time Main Street was going to take Wall Street. So Barry had his brothers, three or four hundred of the hardest delegates in the land, and they were ready to become the lifelong enemy of any delegate who might waver to Scranton.

That was the mood. That was the inner condition of the Goldwater delegates about the time Scranton announced he was going all out for the nomination and would pry these people loose from Barry. Henry Cabot Lodge came in from Vietnam. He was, you remember, going to help. Cynics in the Establishment were quick to inform you that Lodge was actually getting the hell out before the roof fell in, but Lodge gave this message to reporters:

> *. . . One of the things that always used to please me about being in Vietnam was the thought that I might as an older man be able to do something to help our soldiers who were out risking their lives.*
>
> *Well, a couple of weeks ago I ran into this captain who was one of the battalion advisors and he said, 'Are you going back to help Governor Scranton?' And I said, 'No.' 'Well,' he said, 'you're not?' He said, 'I think you ought to.'*
>
> *Well, that gave me quite a – that startled me, rather, because his attitude was: 'I'm doing my duty out here, you'd better get back and do your duty pretty fast.'*

Obviously, no one had ever told Henry Cabot Lodge he might not necessarily be superb. So he came in, kingpin, boy, and symbol of the Establishment, and for two weeks he worked for Scranton (although most curiously – for Lodge was back in America a week before he even made arrangements to meet with Scranton). Still, Lodge announced his readiness to be first target of the Wasp Mafia. At the end of two weeks of picking up the telephone to call old friends only to have the telephone come back in the negative, Lodge looked like a man who had been handsome once. His color was a dirty wax yellow, his smile went up over the gums at the corner of his mouth and gave a hint of the skull the way ninety-year-old men look when their smile goes past the teeth. He looked like they had been beating him in the kidneys with his own liver. It was possible something had been beaten out of him forever.

Of course this was Sunday night – the first session of the convention was not ten hours off on Monday morning – and Scranton and Lodge had had a ferocious bad Sunday; the particular letter inviting Goldwater to debate Scranton before the convention had gone out earlier that day above the Governor's signature and it had gone so far as this:

> *Your managers say in effect that the delegates are little more than a flock of chickens whose necks will be wrung at will ... Goldwaterism has come to stand for a whole crazy-quilt collection of absurd and dangerous positions that would be soundly repudiated by the American people in November.*

Denison Kitchel, Goldwater's General Director of the National Goldwater for President Committee, issued a statement:

> *Governor Scranton's letter has been read here with amazement. It has been returned to him.*
>
> *Perhaps, upon consideration, the Governor will recognize the intemperate nature of his remarks. As it stands, they tragically reflect upon the Republican Party and upon every delegate to the convention.*

Then Kitchel sent out mimeographed copies of Scranton's letter and his own reply to every Republican delegate. The Scranton mine caved in. Flooding at one end of the shaft, it was now burning at the other. Delegates do not like to be told they are a flock of chickens. It is one of those metaphors which fit like a sliver of bone up the nostril. Scranton was to repudiate his letter the following day; he accepted responsibility but disowned the letter – the language was not his – which is to say he admitted he could not run a competent organization. Nor, it developed, could he protect his own people: the name of the assistant who had actually written the letter slipped out quick enough.

Thus, one night before the convention, the letter public, Scranton may just conceivably have moved from deep depression to outright agony. The Republicans were having a Gala that night, five hundred dollars a plate for funds, the press not admitted, although many, some from the front, some from the rear, found a way in, and all the Republican luminaries were there, Eisenhower, and the Luces, Mrs Eisenhower, Henry Cabot Lodge, Thruston Morton, George Murphy, Ray Bliss, Mrs Goldwater, Scranton. All but Barry. In a much-announced rage about the letter, Goldwater was boycotting the Gala. Of course, it was essentially an Establishment Gala, that slowly came clear, and therefore was in degree a wake – news of the letter was passing around. The dance floor was not to be crowded this night.

Scranton came in. He walked down the center aisle between the tables looking like one of the walking wounded. People came up to greet him and he smiled wanly and sadly and a little stiffly as if he were very weary indeed, as if he had just committed hara-kiri but was still walking. When introduced, he said with wan humor, 'I've read your books' – something finally splendid about Scranton.

A minute later, Scranton and Eisenhower came together. It was their first meeting in San Francisco; the General had just arrived that day, come into the Santa Fe depot after crossing the country by train. He was Scranton's last hope;

he might still give momentum to the bogged-down tanks of Scranton's attack – what, after all, was the measure of magic? So Scranton must have looked for every clue in Eisenhower's greeting. There were clues running all over. Ike stood up from his table, he pumped Scranton's hand, he held his elbow, he wheeled about him, he grinned, he smiled widely, he grinned again, his face flushed red, red as a two-week-old infant's face, his eyes twinkled, he never stopped talking, he never took his hands off Scranton, he never looked him in the eye. It was the greeting of a man who is not going to help another man.

Next day, Eisenhower dropped William Warren Scranton. He had a press conference at the Hilton in which he succeeded in saying nothing. It was obvious now he would not come out for anyone, it was also obvious he would not join the Moderates' call for a stronger civil-rights plank. 'Well,' he said, 'he [Melvin Laird] came to see me, and the way he explained it to me, it sounded all right.' Asked about an amendment the Moderates wished to put in the plank, 'The authority to use America's nuclear weapons belongs to the President of the United States,' Eisenhower thought 'this statement was perfectly all right with me because it reaffirms what the Constitution means.' Still he would not fight for it. Asked how he reacted to the idea of a debate before the entire convention between Senator Goldwater and Governor Scranton, a reference directed to Scranton's now famous letter of the day before, Eisenhower said, 'This, of course, would be a precedent, and I am not against precedents. I am not particularly for them.' A little earlier he had said, 'I really have no feeling of my own.' He didn't. He was in a private pond. He had been in one for years. Something had been dying in him for years, the proportions and magnitude of his own death no doubt, and he was going down into the cruelest of fates for an old man, he was hooked on love like an addict, not large love, but the kind of mild tolerant love which shields an old man from hatred. It was obvious that Eisenhower had a deep fear of the forces which were for Goldwater. He did not mind with full pride any longer if people felt contempt for him, but he did not want to be hated hard by anyone. So he could not declare himself, not for anything, and as he made his lapses in syntax, in word orders, in pronunciations, they took on more prominence than they ever had. At times, they were as rhythmic as a tic, or a dog scratching at a bite. He would say, 'We must be objec*tive*, I mean ob*jec*tive, we must be objective . . .' and on he would go as if he were sinking very slowly and quietly into the waters of his future death which might be a year away or ten years away but was receiving him nonetheless like a marsh into which he disappeared twitch by twitch, some beating of wet wings against his fate.

° . . . Looke, Lord, and finde both Adams met in me.'
                                                    – JOHN DONNE

Now, as for Goldwater, he had dimensions. Perhaps they were no more than contradictions, but he was not an easy man to comprehend in a hurry. His wife, for example, had been at the Gala, sitting with some family and friends, but at one of the less agreeable tables on the floor, off to the side and sufficiently back of the stage so that you could not see the entertainer. It seemed a curious way for the Establishment to treat the wife of the leading contender, but I was assured by the young lady who brought me over for the introduction that Mrs Goldwater preferred it that way. 'She hates being the center of attention,' I was told. Well, she turned out to be a shy attractive woman with a gentle not altogether happy but sensual face. There was something nice about her and very vulnerable. He eyes were moist, they were luminous. It was impossible not to like her. Whereas her daughters were attractive in a different fashion. 'I want the best ring in this joint, buster,' I could hear them say.

Goldwater's headquarters, however, were at a remove from the ladies. Occupying the fourteenth and fifteenth floors of the Mark Hopkins, they were not easy to enter. The main elevators required a wait of forty-five minutes to go up. The alternate route was off the mezzanine through a pantry onto a service car. A half-filled twenty-gallon garbage can stood by the service-elevator door. You went squeezed up tight with high and low honchos for Goldwater, plus waiters with rolling carts working room service. Once there, the fourteenth and fifteenth floors were filthy. A political headquarters is never clean – stacks of paper, squeezed-out paper cups, typewriter carbons on the floor, jackets on wire hangers all angles on a rack – a political headquarters is like the City Room of a newspaper. But Goldwater's headquarters were filthier than most. There was a general detritus like the high-water mark on a beach. The armchairs were dusty and the sofas looked like hundred-dollar newlywed sofas dirty in a day. The air had the beat-out cigar smell of the waiting room in a large railroad station. It had nothing to do with the personnel. No one on the fourteenth or fifteenth floor had anything to do with his surroundings. You could have dropped them in Nymphenburg or a fleabag off Eighth Avenue – the rooms would come to look the same. A room was a place with a desk where the work got out.

They had something in common – professional workers for Goldwater – something not easy to define. They were not like the kids out in the street, nor did they have much in common with the old cancer-guns in the lobby; no, the worst of these workers looked like divinity students who had been expelled from the seminary for embezzling class funds and still felt they were nearest to J.C. – there was a dark blank fanaticism in their eyes. And the best of the Goldwater professionals were formidable, big rangy men, some lean, some flabby, with the hard distasteful look of topflight investigators for fire-insurance companies, field men for the F.B.I., or like bright young district attorneys, that lean flat look of the hunter, full of moral indignation and moral vacuity. But the total of all the professional Goldwater people one saw on the fourteenth and fifteenth floors was directly reminiscent of a guided tour through the F.B.I. in the Department of Justice Building in Washington, that same succession of handsome dull faces for guide, hair combed straight back or combed straight from a part, eyes lead shot, noses which offered nothing, mouths which were functional, good chins, deft moves. A succession of these men took the tourists through the halls of the F.B.I. and read aloud the signs on the exhibits for us and gave short lectures about the function of the F.B.I. (guard us from the enemy without, the enemy within, Communism and Crime – the statements offered in simple organizational prose of the sort used in pamphlets which welcome new workers to large corporations, soldiers to new commands, freshmen to high school, and magazine readers to editorials). The tourists were mainly fathers and sons. The wives were rugged, the kind who are built for dungarees and a green plaid hunting jacket, the sisters and daughters plain and skinny, no expression. They all had lead shot for eyes, the lecturers and the tourists. Most of the boys were near twelve and almost without exception had the blank private faces which belong to kids who kill their old man with a blast, old lady with a butcher's knife, tie sister with telephone cord and hide out in the woods for three days. The climax of the tour was a demonstration by the F.B.I. agent how to use a tommy gun. For ten minutes he stitched targets, using one shot at a time, bursts of three, full magazine, he did it with the mild grace of a body-worker hitting small rivets, there was solemn applause after each burst of shots.

That was a part of the Republic, and here it was at Headquarters for Goldwater. The faces in these rooms were the cream of the tourists and the run of the F.B.I.; there was a mood like the inside of a prison: enclosed air, buried urgency. But that was not altogether fair. The sense of a prison could come from the number of guards and the quality of their style. They were tough dull Pinkertons with a tendency to lean on a new visitor. One desire came off them. They would not be happy if there were no orders to follow. With orders, they were ready to put the arm on Bill Scranton, Nelson Rockefeller, or General Eisenhower (if told to). Probably they would put the arm on Johnson if he appeared and was ordered out. Naturally they were not there for that, they were there to defend Headquarters from mobs (read: niggers) and the Senator from black assassination. It made sense up to a point: Goldwater was in more danger than Scranton, at least so long as Scranton showed no sign of winning; just that day, Sunday, there had been a civil-rights anti-Goldwater march down Market Street. The heavy protection was nonetheless a fraud. No mob was getting to the fourteenth floor, nor to Goldwater's fort on the fifteenth (a separate barricade of Pinkertons guarded the twenty-odd steps), no mob was going to get all the way up with just those three elevators and a wait of forty-five units of sixty seconds each, no assassin was likely to try Headquarters when there were opportunities on the street; no, the atmosphere was created to create atmosphere, the aura at Headquarters was solemnity, debris underfoot, and grave decisions, powers put to the service of order, some conspiracy of the vault, a dedication to the necessity of taking power. That was Headquarters. One never got to see Goldwater in the place.

There was opportunity, however, to come within three feet of him later that day, once at the caucus of the Florida delegation in the Beverly Plaza, once on the street moving from hotel to hotel (Pinkertons no longer in evidence now – just cops) and again at the Clift, where he talked to the Washington delegation. There was excitement watching Barry go to work with a group, an intensity in the air, a religious devotion, as if one of the most urbane priests of America was talking at a Communion breakfast, or as if the Principal-of-the-Year was having a heart-to-heart with honor students. The Florida delegation, meeting in a dingy little downstairs banquet room, was jammed. The afternoon had turned hot for San Francisco. Eighty degrees outside, it may have been ninety in the room. Everybody was perspiring. Barry sat in the front, a spotlight on him, a silver film of perspiration adding to his patina, and the glasses, those black-framed glasses, took on that odd life of their own, that pinched severity, that uncompromising idealism which made Goldwater kin to the tight-mouthed and the lonely. Talking in a soft modest voice, he radiated at this moment the skinny boyish sincerity of a fellow who wears glasses but is determined nonetheless to have a good time. Against all odds. It was not unreminiscent of Arthur Miller: that same mixture of vast solemnity and unspoiled boyhood, a sort of shucks and aw shit in the voice. 'Well, you see,' said Goldwater, talking to the Florida delegation, 'if I was to trust the polls right now, I'd have to say I didn't have a chance. But why should I trust the polls? Why should any of us trust the polls? They've been wrong before. They'll be wrong again. Man is superior to the machine. The thing to remember is that America is a spiritual country, we're founded on belief in God, we may wander a little as a country, but we never get too far away. I'm ready to say the election is going to give the Democrats a heck of a surprise. Why, I'll tell you this,' Goldwater said, sweating mildly, telling the folks from Florida just as keen if he was alone with each one of them, each one of these elderly gents and real-estate dealers and plain women with silver-rimmed eyeglasses, 'tell you this, I'm doing my best not to keep this idea a secret, but I think we're not only going to give the Democrats a heck of a surprise, I think we're going to win. [Applause, cheers.] In fact I wouldn't be in this if I didn't think we were going to win. [Applause.] Why, as I sometimes tell my wife, I'm too young to retire and too old to go back to work.' [Laughter, loud cheers.] Goldwater was done. He smiled shyly, his glasses saying: I am a modest man, and I am severe on myself. As he made his route to the door, the delegates were touching him enthusiastically.

Back on the street – he was walking the blocks to the

Hotel Clift where the Washington State delegation was having a Goldwater reception – his tail consisted of fifty or sixty excited people, some Florida delegates who didn't wish to lose sight of the man, plus a couple of cops glad to have the duty. Cars slowed down to look at him; one stopped. A good-looking woman got out and cheered. There was something in the way she did it. Just as strange Negroes scattered at random through a white audience may act in awareness of one another, so the Goldwater supporters in their thirties and forties gave off a similar confidence of holding the secret. This very good-looking woman yelled, 'You go, Barry, you go, go.' But there was anger and elation in her voice, as if she were declaring, 'We're going to get the country back.' And Goldwater smiled modestly and went on. He looked a little in fever. Small wonder. He could be President of the United States in less than half a year, he could stop a sniper's bullet he never knew when, he was more loved and hated than any man in America, and inside all these was just *him*, the man who adjusted radio knobs in the early morning in order to transmit a little better, and now conceivably adjusted a few knobs . . .

At the Hotel Clift he talked to the Washington delegates. We were definitely back in high school. That was part of Goldwater's deal – he brought you back to the bright minted certitudes of early patriotism when you knew the U.S. was the best country on earth and there was no other. Yes, his appeal would go out to all the millions who were now starved and a little sour because some part of their life had ended in high school, and the university they had never seen. But then Barry had had but one year of college – he had indeed the mind of a powerful freshman. 'I want to thank you folks from Washington for giving me this warm greeting. Of course, Washington is the name of a place I often like to get the heck out of, but I'm sure I won't confuse the two right here.' [Laughter.] He was off, a short political speech. In the middle, extremism. 'I don't know how anybody can be an extremist who believes in the Constitution. And for

those misguided few who pretend to believe in the Con-
stitution, but in secret don't, well they may be extremists,
but I don't see any necessity to legislate against them. I just
feel sorry for them.' [Cheers. Applause. Happiness at the
way Barry delivered anathemas.] At a certain point in the
speech, he saw a woman in the audience whom he recog-
nized, and stopped in the middle of a phrase. 'Hi, honey,' he
sang out like a traveling salesman, which brought a titter
from the delegation, for his voice had shifted too quickly,
the codpiece was coming off, Rain and the Reverend David-
son. Something skinny, itchy, hard as a horselaugh, showed
– he was a cannoneer with a hairy ear. Goldwater went on,
the good mood continued; then at the end, speech done, he
turned down a drink but said in his best gee-whizzer, 'I'm
sorry I have to leave because gosh I'd like to break a few
with you.' Laughter, and he took off head down, a little
modest in the exit, a little red in the neck.

There was entertainment at the Republican Gala on
Sunday night. The climax was a full marching band of bag-
pipers. They must have been hired for the week since one
kept hearing them on the following days, and at all odd
times, heard them even in my hotel room at four a.m., for a
few were marching in the streets of San Francisco, sounding
through the night, giving off the barbaric evocation of the
Scots, all valor, wrath, firmitude, and treachery – the wild
complete treachery of the Scots finding its way into the
sound of the pipes. They were a warning of the fever in the
heart of the Wasp. There are sounds which seem to pass
through all the protective gates in the ear and reach into
some nerve where the eschatology is stored. Few parents
have failed to hear it in the cry of their infant through the
morning hours or a bad night – stubbornness, fury, waste, and
the promise of revenge come out of a flesh half-created by
one's own flesh; the knowledge is suddenly there that seed is
existential, no paradise resides in seed, seed can be ill-
inspired and go to a foul gloomy end. Some find their part of
the truth in listening to jazz – it is moot if any white who had

no ear for jazz can know the passion with which some whites become attached to the Negro's cause. So, too, listening to the bagpipes, you knew this was the true music of the Wasps. There was something wild and martial and bottomless in the passion, a pride which would not be exhausted, a determination which might never end, perhaps should never end, the Faustian rage of a white civilization was in those Highland wails, the cry of a race which was born to dominate and might never learn to share, and never learning, might be willing to end the game, the end of the world was in the sound of the pipes. Or at very least the danger one would come closer to the world's end. So there was a vast if all-private appeal in listening to the pipes shrill out the herald of a new crusade, something jagged, Viking, of the North in the air, a sense of breaking ice and barbaric shields, hunters loose in the land again. And this had an appeal which burrowed deep, there was excitement at the thought of Goldwater getting the nomination, as if now finally all one's personal suicides, all the deaths of the soul accumulated by the past, all the failures, all the terrors, could find purge in a national situation where a national murder was being planned (the Third World War) and one's own suicide might be lost in a national suicide. There was that excitement, that the burden of one's soul (always equal to the burden of one's personal responsibility) might finally be lifted – what a release was there! Beauty was inspired by the prospect. For if Goldwater won, and the iron power of the iron people who had pushed him forth – as echoed in the iron of the Pinkertons on the fourteenth and fifteenth floor – now pushed forth over the nation an iron regime with totalitarianism seizing the TV in every frozen dinner, well then at last a true underground might form; and liberty at the thought of any catalyst which could bring it on. Yes, the Goldwater movement excited the depths because the apocalypse was brought more near, and like millions of other whites, I had been leading a life which was a trifle too pointless and a trifle too full of guilt and my gullet was close to nausea with the endless compromises of an empty liberal center. So I followed the four days of the convention with something more than simple apprehension. The country was taking a turn, the colors were deepening, the knives of the afternoon were out, something of the best in American life might now be going forever; or was it altogether to the opposite? And was the country starting at last to take the knots of its contradictions up from a premature midnight of nightmare into the surgical terrains of the open skin? Were we in the beginning, or turning the middle, of our worst disease? One did not know any longer, you simply did not know any longer, but something was certain: the country was now part of the daily concern. One worried about it for the first time, the way you worried about family or work, a good friend or the future, and that was the most exceptional of emotions.

II

'. . . When men are too much confined to professional and faculty habits, and as it were inveterate in the recurrent employment of that narrow circle, they are rather disabled than qualified for whatever depends on the knowledge of mankind, on experience in mixed affairs, on a comprehensive, connected view of the various, complicated, external and internal interests, which go to the formation of that multifarious thing called a state.'

— BURKE, *Reflections on the Revolution in France*

If the details of the Republican convention of 1964 were steeped in concern, it was nonetheless not very exciting, not technically. As a big football game, the score might have been 76 to 0, or 76 to 3. (There were sentimentalists who would claim that Rockefeller kicked a field goal.) Compared however to the Republican Convention of 1940 when Wendell Wilkie came from behind to sweep the nomination on the sixth ballot, or the 1952 convention when Eisenhower defeated Taft on the second roll call of the states, compared even to the Democratic Convention of 1960, there were few moments in this affair, and nothing even remotely comparable in excitement to the demonstration for Adlai Stevenson four years ago when Eugene McCarthy put him in nomination. Yet this convention of 1964 would remain as one of the most important in our history; it took place with religious exaltation for some, with dread for others, and in sheer trauma for the majority of the Press and Television who were present on the scene. For them it offered four days of anxiety as pure and deep as a child left alone in a house. The purpose of the press in America has been to tinker with the machine, to adjust, to prepare a seat for new valves and values, to lubricate, to excuse, to justify, to serve in the maintenance of the Establishment. From I. F. Stone on the left, going far to the right of Joseph Alsop, over almost so far as David Lawrence, the essential understanding of the mass media is that the machine of the nation is a muddle which is endlessly grateful for ministrations of the intellect; so a game is played in which the Establishment always forgives the mass media for its excesses, and the mass media brings its sense of civilization (adjustment, psychoanalysis, responsibility, and the milder shores of love) to the service of the family Establishment. Virtually everything is forgiven by both sides. The contradictory remarks of politicians are forgotten, the more asinine predictions of pundits are buried with mercy. The Establishment for example would not remind Joe Alsop that in March 1964 he had written, 'No serious Republican politician, even of the most Neanderthal type, any longer takes Goldwater seriously.' No, the Press was not to be twitted for the limits of their technique because half their comprehension of the nation derived after all from material supplied by the Establishment; the other half came from conversations with each other. All too often the Press lives in the investigative condition of a lover who performs the act for two minutes a day and talks about it for twenty hours of the twenty-four. So a daisy chain like the

National Review proves to be right about Goldwater's strength and the intellectual Establishment with its corporate resources is deep in error.

An explanation? Those who hold power think the devil is best contained by not mentioning his name. This procedure offers a formidable shell in which to live, but its cost is high; the housing is too ready to collapse when the devil decides to show. There has been no opportunity to study him. Just as a generation of the Left, stifled and ignored through the McCarthyism of the Fifties and the Eisenhowerism of the Fifties, caused panic everywhere when they emerged as the Beat Generation, so another generation, a generation of the Right, has been stifled, their actions reported inaccurately, their remarks distorted, their ideals (such as they are) ignored, and their personal power underestimated. The difference however is that the Beat Generation was a new flock of early Christians gathered prematurely before the bomb, an open-air asylum for the gentle and the mad, where in contrast the underground generation of the Right is a frustrated posse, a convention of hangmen who subscribe to the principle that the executioner has his rights as well. The liberal mind collapses before this notion but half of nature may be contained in the idea that the weak are happiest when death is quick. It is a notion which since the Nazis has been altogether detestable, but then the greatest intellectual damage the Nazis may have done was to take a few principles from nature and pervert them root and nerve. In the name of barbarism and a return to primitive health they accelerated the most total and surrealistic aspects of civilization. The gas chamber was a full albino descendant of the industrial revolution.

But that is a digression. To return to the yet milder political currents of the Left and the Right in America, one could say the Beat Generation was a modest revolution, suicidal in the center of its passion. At its most militant it wished for immolation rather than power, it desired only to be left free enough to consume itself. Yet in the mid-Fifties liberals reacted with a profound terror, contumely, and ridicule to its manifestations as if their own collective suicide (the private terror of the liberal spirit is invariably suicide, not murder) was to be found in the gesture of the Beat. What then the panic of the liberal Establishment before a revolution of the Right whose personal nightmare might well be their inability to contain their most murderous impulse, a movement of the Right whose ghost is that unlaid blood and breath of Nazism which has hovered these twenty years like a succubus over the washed-out tissues of civilization. Consider but one evidence of the fear: that part of the Press called Periodicals sat in a section of the gallery to the left of the speakers in the Cow Palace. There were one hundred writers in this Periodical section of the gallery and six passes to get down to the floor where one could talk to delegates and in turn be looked at by them. Of those six passes, one or two were always available. Which meant that the majority of writers did not try to get down to the floor very often. Sitting next to one another the writers were content to observe – there were killers on the floor.

There were. It was a convention murderous in mood. The mood of this convention spoke of a new kind of society. Chimeras of fascism hung like fogbank. And high enthusiasm. Some of the delegates were very happy. '*Viva,*' would shout a part of the gallery. '*Olé,*' would come the answer. There was an éclat, a bull roar, a mystical communion in the sound even as *Sieg Heil* used to offer its mystical communion. *Viva-Olé.* Live-Yay! Live-Yay! It was the new chic of the mindless. The American mind had gone from Hawthorne and Emerson to the Frug, the Bounce, and Walking the Dog, from *The Flowering of New England* to the cerebrality of professional football in which a quarterback must have not only heart, courage, strength and grace but a mind like an I.B.M. computer. It marks the turn we have taken from the Renaissance. There too was the ideal of a hero with heart, courage, strength, and grace, but he was expected to possess the mind of a passionate artist. Now the

best heroes were – in the sense of the Renaissance – mind-
less: Y. A. Tittle, John Glenn, Tracy, Smiling Jack; the
passionate artists were out on the hot rods, the twist band was
whipping the lovers, patriotism was a football game, a fas-
cism would come in (if it came) on Live-Yay! Let's live-yay!
The hype had made fifty million musical-comedy minds;
now the hype could do anything; it could set high-school
students to roar *Viva-Olé*, and they would roar it while
victims of a new totalitarianism would be whisked away to a
new kind of camp – hey, honey, do you twist, they would
yell into the buses.

*'When men of rank sacrifice all ideas of dignity to an ambition
without a distinct object, and work with low instruments and
for low ends, the whole composition becomes low and base.'*

          –BURKE, *Reflections on the Revolution in France*

First major event of the convention was Eisenhower's ap-
pearance at the Cow Palace to give a speech on Tuesday
afternoon. The arena was well-chosen for a convention.
Built in the Thirties when indoor sports stadiums did not yet
look like children's nurseries, the Cow Palace offered echoes
– good welterweights and middleweights had fought here,
there was iron in the air. And the Republicans had installed
the speaker's platform at one end of the oval; the delegates
sat therefore in a file which was considerably longer than it
was wide, the speaker was thus installed at the handle of the
sword. (Whereas the Democrats in 1960 had put the speaker
in the middle of the oval.) But this was the part after all of
Republican fathers rather than Democratic mothers. If there
were any delegates to miss the psychic effect of this decision,
a huge banner raised behind the speaker confronted them
with the legend: Of the people, By the people, For the
people. 'Of the people' was almost invisible; 'By the people'
was somewhat more clear; 'For the people' was loud and
strong. This was a party not much 'of the people' but very
much 'for the people', it presumed to know what was good
for them.

And for fact, that had always been Ike's poor lone strength as a speaker, he knew what was good for you. He dipped into his speech, 'here with great pride because I am a Republican,' 'my deep dedication to Republicanism' – he had not been outward bound for five minutes before the gallery was yawning. Ike had always been a bore, but there had been fascination in the boredom when he was President – this, after all, was *the* man. Now he was just another hog wrassler of rhetoric; he pinned a few phrases in his neat determined little voice, and a few phrases pinned him back. Ike usually fought a speech to a draw. It was hard to listen. All suspense had ended at Monday morning's Press Conference. Ike would not come out in support of Scranton. So the mind of the Press drifted out with the mind of the gallery. If Ike said a few strong words about the Civil Rights Bill – 'Republicans in Congress to their great credit voted far more overwhelmingly than did our opponents to pass the Civil Rights Bill' – it meant nothing. The Moderates tried to whoop it up, the Goldwater delegations looked on in ranked masses of silence. Ike went on. He gave the sort of speech which takes four or five columns in the *New York Times* and serves to clot the aisles of history. He was still, as he had been when he was President, a cross between a boy and an old retainer. The boy talked, earnest, innocent, a high-school valedictorian debating the affirmative of, Resolved: Capitalism is the Most Democratic System on Earth; and the old retainer quavered into the voice, the old retainer could no longer live without love.

Ike had bored many a crowd in his time. He had never bored one completely – he had always known how to get some token from a mob. Ever since 1952, he had been giving little pieces of his soul to draw demonstrations from the mob. You could always tell the moment. His voice shifted. Whenever he was ready to please the crowd, he would warn them by beginning to speak with a brisk little anger. Now it came, now he said it. '... Let us particularly scorn the *divisive* efforts of those outside our family, including sensation-seeking columnists and commentators [beginning of a wild demonstration] because,' said Ike, his voice showing a glint of full spite, 'I assure you that these are people who couldn't care less about the good of our party.' He was right, of course. That was not why he said it, however; he said it to repay the Press for what they had said about him these last three weeks; the sensation they had been seeking was – so far as he was concerned – to arouse needles of fury in an old man's body – he said what he said for revenge. Mainly he said it to please the Goldwater crowd, there was the hint of that in his voice. The Goldwater delegations and the gallery went into the first large demonstration of the convention. Trumpets sounded, heralds of a new crusade: cockroaches, columnists, and Communists to be exterminated. There were reports in the papers next day that delegates shook their fists at newspapermen on the floor, and at the television men with their microphones. The mass media is of course equipped for no such war. Some of the men from the mass media looked like moon men: they wore red helmets and staggered under the load of a portable camera which must have weighed fifty pounds and was packed on their back; others of the commentators had portable mikes and hats with antennae. To the delegates they must have looked like insects grown to the size of a man. Word whipped in to the delegations from the all-call telephone in the office trailer of the Goldwater command post back of the Cow Palace. Cut the demonstration, was the word from F. Clifton White. The demonstration subsided. But the Press did not, the rest of the mass media did not. They remained in a state of agitation: if Ike was ready to accuse, anyone could serve as hangman. Anyone would. Anyone they knew.

Much later that Tuesday, after the full reading of the full platform, came a debate between the Moderates and the Conservatives. Success in politics comes from putting one's seat to a chair and sitting through dull wrangles in order to be present after midnight when the clubhouse vote is cast. Playboys do not go far in these circumstances, nor adventurers; the mediocre recognized early that a society was evolving which would enable them to employ the very vice which hitherto had made life intolerable – mediocrity itself. So the cowardly took their place in power. They had the superior ability to breathe in hours of boredom.

Politics was now open however to the disease of the bored – magic. Magic can sweep you away. Once a decade, once every two decades, like a big wind which eludes the weather charts and seems to arise from the caverns of the ocean itself, so does a hurricane sweep a convention. It happened with Wendell Willkie in 1940; it flickered on the horizon with Stevenson in '60; it was Scranton's hope to work a real debate on the last session before the balloting. If he could win even once on some small point, rumors of magic could arise. The Moderates had forced therefore a floor fight to propose a few amendments to the Republican platform of '64. One: that only the President have the authority to use America's nuclear weapons. Two: repudiate the John Birch Society. Three: introduce a language of approval for the Civil Rights Act. The chances of success were small at best: only an extraordinary assault on the emotions of the Goldwater delegations could sway them to vote yes for the amendments.

The Moderates however went to battle moderately. Their speakers were impressive (as such a quality is measured in the *Times*). They were Christian Herter, Hugh Scott, Clifford Case, George Romney, Lindsay, Javits, Rockefeller. They were not, however, lively speakers, not this night. Lindsay and Javits were presentable in professional groups; devoted to detailed matters, they spoke with reason; Case spoke like a shy high-school teacher; Christian Herter was reminiscent of Mr Chips; Hugh Scott owned no fire. Carlino (Majority Leader in the New York Assembly) sounded like a successful restaurant owner. And Governor Romney of Michigan had his own special amendments, he was a moderation of the moderates. As he spoke, he looked like a handsome version of Boris Karloff, all honesty, big-jawed, soft-eyed, eighty days at sea on a cockeyed passion. He spoke in a loud strong voice yet one sensed a yaw at the center of his brain which left his celebrations as lost as Karloff's lost little voice. No, the only excitement had come at the beginning. Rockefeller was not a man who would normally inspire warmth. He had a strong decent face and something tough as the rubber in a handball to his makeup, but his eyes had been punched out a long time ago – they had the distant lunar glow of the small sad eyes you see in a caged chimpanzee or gorilla. Even when hearty he gave an impression the private man was remote as an astronaut on a lost orbit. But Rockefeller had his ten minutes at the podium and as he talked of suffering 'at first-hand' in the California primary from the methods of 'extremist elements', threatening letters unsigned, bomb threats, 'threat of personal violence', telephone calls, 'smear and hate literature', 'strong-arm and goon tactics,' the gallery erupted, and the boos and jeers came down. Rockefeller could have been Leo Durocher walking out to the plate at Ebbets Field to protest an umpire's decision after Leo had moved from the Dodgers to the Giants. Again the all-call in the Goldwater trailer outside the Cow Palace was busy, again the delegations were told to be silent, and obeyed. But the gallery would not stop, and Thruston Morton, the Chairman, came forward like one of the sweepers in *Camino Real* to tell Kilroy his time was up. Rockefeller had his moment. 'You quiet them,' he said to Morton. 'That's your job. I want my time to speak.' And there was a conception of Rockefeller finally – he had few ideas and none of them were his own, he had a personality which was never in high focus (in the sense that Bobby Kennedy and Jimmy Hoffa are always in high focus) but he had an odd courage which was profound – he could take strength from defying a mob. Three hundred thousand years ago, a million years ago, some gorilla must have stood up to an enraged tribe and bellowed back and got away alive and human society was begun. So Rocky finally had his political moment which was precisely right for him.

But the other Moderates did not. There was in their collective voice a suggestion of apology: let-us-at-least-be-heard. Speakers who were opposed to the amendments sounded as effective, sometimes more. Ford from Michigan spoke after Rockefeller, and had better arguments. It was not, he suggested, the purpose of a party which believed in free speech to look for formulas to repress opinion. He was right, even if he might not be so ready to protect Communists as Reactionaries. And Senator Dominick of Colorado made a bright speech employing an editorial from the *New York Times* of 1765 which rebuked Patrick Henry for extreme ideas. Delegates and gallery whooped it up. Next day Dominick confessed. He was only 'spoofing'. He had known: there was no *New York Times* in 1765. Nor was there any editorial. An old debater's trick. If there are no good facts, make them up. Be quick to write your own statistics. There was some umbilical tie between the Right Wing and the psychopathic liar.

More speakers came on. After four or five speakers for each side, a vote would come. Each time the amendment was voted down. Eight hundred and ninety-so-many to four hundred-and-a-few, went the votes. Hours went by, three hours of debate. After a while, the Moderates came collectively to seem like a club fighter in still another loser. A vacuum hung over empty cries for civil rights. One wondered why a Negro delegate loyal to the Party for thirty years had not been asked by the Moderates to make a speech where he could say: *You are sending me home to my people a mockery and a shame. My people have been saying for thirty years that the Republican Party has no love for the colored man, and I have argued back. Tonight you will tell me I was wrong. You are denying me the meaning of my life.*

Such a speech (and there were Negro delegates to give it) might not have turned the vote, doubtless it would not have turned the vote, but it was the Moderates' sole chance for an explosion which could loose some petrified emotion, some magic. They did not take it. Probably they did not take it because they did not care that much if they lost. By now, it might be better to lose decisively than come nearer to winning and divide the party more. So they accepted their loser's share of the purse, which is that they could go back East and say: I campaigned at the convention for Civil Rights. Tomorrow was nominating day. The last chance in a hundred had been lost.

> *The Bleat, the Bark, Bellow & Roar—*
> *Are Waves that Beat on Heaven's Shore . . .*
>
> —WILLIAM BLAKE, *Auguries of Innocence*

Everett Dirksen gave the nominating speech for Goldwater, Dirksen from Illinois, the Silver Fox of the Senate, the Minority Leader, the man who had done the most, many would claim, to pass the Civil Rights Bill, for it was his coalition with Hubert Humphrey on cloture which had carried the day. 'I guess Dirksen finally got religion,' Humphrey said, and Dirksen, making his final speech for the bill, declared, 'There is no force so powerful as an idea whose time has come.' It was said that when Goldwater voted against the bill, Dirksen would not speak to him. Two weeks later, Dirksen agreed to nominate Goldwater. 'He's got it won, that's all,' Dirksen said of Goldwater, 'this thing has gone too far.'

This day, nominating day, any orator could have set fire to the Cow Palace. The gallery and Goldwater delegations were as tense and impatient as a platoon of Marines going down to Tijuana after three weeks in the field. But this day Dirksen had no silver voice. He made a speech which contained such nuggets as, 'In an age of do-gooders, he was a good doer.' Dirksen was an old organist who would play all the squeaks in all the stops, rustle over all the dead bones of all the dead mice in all the pipes. He naturally made a large point that Barry Goldwater was 'the grandson of the peddler.' This brought no pleasure to the crowd. Main Street was taking Wall Street; Newport Beach, California, would replace Newport; and General Goldwater, Air Force Reserve, possessed sufficient cachet to negotiate the move; but not the grandson of the peddler. Dirksen however went on and on, making a sound like the whir of the air conditioning in a two-mile tunnel.

When he was done, they blew Dirksen down, the high screams of New Year's Eve went off, a din of screamers, rattles, and toots, a clash of bands, a dazzle of posters in phosphorescent yellow and orange and gold, the mad prance of the state standards, wild triumphant pokes and jiggles, war spears, crusaders' lances, an animal growl of joy, rebel cries, eyes burning, a mad nut in each square jaw, *Viva-Olé, Viva-Olé*, bugle blasts and rallying cries, the call of heralds, and a fall from the rafters of a long golden rain, pieces of gold foil one inch square, hundreds of thousands of such pieces in an endless gentle shimmer of descent. They had put a spot on the fall – it was as if sunlight had entered every drop of a fine sweet rain. I ran into Mike Wallace on the floor. 'The guy who thought of this was a genius,' said Mike. And the sounds of the band went up to meet the rain. There was an unmistakable air of beauty, as if a rainbow had come to a field of war, or Goths around a fire saw visions in a cave. The heart of the beast had loosed a primitive call. Civilization was worn thin in the center and to the Left the black man raised his primitive cry; now to the far Right were the maniacal blue eyes of the other primitive. The jungles and the forests were readying for war. It was certain beyond certainty now that America was off on a ride which would end – was it God or the Devil knew where.

But the ride did not begin for another seven hours and seven nominations. Knowland seconded Goldwater's nomination; and Clare Boothe Luce, Charlie Halleck, Senator Tower. Then Keating nominated Rockefeller, a twenty-two-minute demonstration, decent in size but predictably hollow. More seconding speeches. Next came Scranton's turn. Dr Milton Eisenhower, Ike's younger brother, did the nominating. It was good, it was clear, but there was not much excitement any more. One knew why the older Eisenhower had wanted the younger Eisenhower to be President. One also knew why he had not come very near – he gave a hint of Woodrow Wilson. Then the demonstration for Scranton. It was respectable, it let loose a half hour of music, it had fervor, the Scranton supporters died pure, an enjoyable demonstration. But the music was softer. Instead of *Viva-Olé* and the bugle blasts and rallying cries of the crusaders, one now heard *Boys and Girls Together*, or *Hail, Hail, the Gang's All Here.* And the Scranton posters did not have the deep yellow and deep orange of the phalanxes who had jammed the gorge for Goldwater; no, they bore blue and red letters on white, or even black on white, a gray photograph of Scranton on a white background with letters in black – the sign had been designed by Brooks Brothers, you may bet. Even some of the lapel buttons for Scranton revealed a camp of understatement, since they were five inches in diameter, yet Scranton's name was in letters one-eighth of an inch high. It made one think of *The New Yorker* and the blank ordered harmoniums of her aisles and text.

Now went the nominations hour after hour like the time between four in the morning and breakfast at a marathon dance. Here came the nominating speeches and the pumped-up state demonstrations on the floor which spoke of plump elderly tourists doing the hula in Hawaii. Then would come a team of seconding speeches, the weepers and the wringers, the proud of nose and the knotty of nose, the kickers and the thumpers, the ministerial bores and the rabbinical drones, the self-satisfied, the glad-to-be-there, the self-anointed, the unctuous, the tooth suckers, the quaverers.

Fong was nominated, and Margaret Chase Smith, first woman ever to be nominated for President. Now she had a lock on the footnotes in the history books. Romney was nominated, and Judd, defeated Congressman Walter H. Judd of Minnesota, given a grand-old-man-of-the-party nominating speech. The band played *Glory, Glory, Hal-*

lelujah. Just after World War II, early in 1946, Judd had been one of the first to talk of war with Russia. Last came Lodge who scratched himself. The nominations were done. The balloting could begin. They cleared the floor of the Press.

We had been there off and on for seven hours, circling the delegations, talking where we could, a secondary sea of locusts. All through the seven hours of this afternoon and evening, there was the California delegation. They could not be ignored. They sat in the front rows off the center aisle just beneath the speaker on the podium. They wore yellow luminescent Goldwater shirts, the sort of sleeveless high-colored shirts which highway workers wear to be phosphorescent at night. On the floor there were a thousand sights and fifty conversations those seven hours, but there was nothing like the California delegation. In California Rockefeller had lost to Goldwater by less than three percent of the vote, and, losing, had lost all the delegates. California had eighty-six delegates – all eighty-six by the rules of the victory were for Goldwater. So there were eighty-six yellow shirts right down front. Winning California, the Right had also won the plums of the convention, the distribution of tickets in the gallery, central placement on the floor, the allegiance of the Cow Palace cops. They had won the right to have their eighty-six faces at the center of the convention.

Most of the California delegation looked like fat state troopers or prison guards or well-established ranchers. A few were thin and looked like Robert Mitchum playing the mad reverend in *Night of the Hunter*. One or two were skinny as Okies, and looked like the kind of skinny wild-eyed gas-station attendant who works in a small town, and gets his picture in the paper because he has just committed murder with a jack handle. Yes, the skinny men in the California delegation leered out wildly. They looked like they were sitting on a body – the corpse of Jew Eastern Negritudes – and when the show was over, they were gonna eat it. That was it – half the faces in the California delegation looked like geeks. They had had it and now they were ready to put fire to the big tent.

There was one man who stood out as their leader – he had the face to be a leader of such men. Of course he looked not at all like a robber baron, the pride of Pinkerton, and a political boss all in one, no, nor was he in the least like an amalgam of Wallace Beery and fat Hermann Goering, no he was just Bill Knowland, ex-Senator William F. Knowland, Lord of the China Lobby, and honcho number one for Barry in Northern and Southern Cal.

So began the balloting. In twenty minutes there was another demonstration. The California standard, a white silk flag with a beast, some mongrel of bear and wild boar, danced in the air as if carried by a knight on a horse. The chairman for South Carolina intoned, 'We are humbly grateful that we can do this for America. South Carolina casts sixteen votes for Senator Barry Goldwater.' Barry was in. Four years of work were over. Final score: 883 for Goldwater. Scranton, 214. Rockefeller had 114, Romney 41. Smith received 27, Judd 22, Lodge 2, and Fong had 5.

When the voting was done, when the deliriums were down, an ooh of pleasure came up from the crowd, like the ooh for an acrobat. For Scranton accompanied by his wife was walking down the ramp to the podium, down the high ramp which led from the end-arena exits to the speaker's stand. It was a walk of a hundred feet or more, and Scranton came down this ramp with a slow measured deferential step, like a boy carrying a ceremonial bowl.

He made a clear speech in a young rather vibrant voice. He was doing the thing he was best at. He was making a gesture his elders would approve. He called on Republicans 'not to desert our party but to strengthen it'.

They cheered him modestly and many may have thought of his comments about Goldwater. On different days through June and July he had said: 'dangerously impulsive', 'spreading havoc across the national landscape', 'a cruel misunderstanding of how the American economy works', 'injurious to innumerable candidates', 'chaos and uproar', 'talking off the top of his head'. 'Hypocrisy . . .' says our friend Burke, 'delights in the most sublime speculations; for never intending to go beyond speculation, it costs nothing to have it magnificent.' 'I ask . . .' Scranton said. He asked his delegates to make Goldwater's nomination unanimous.

Anywhere but in politics the speed with which the position had been shifted would be sign of a monumental instability. But politics was the place where finally nobody meant what they said – it was a world of nightmare; psychopaths roved. The profound and searing conflicts of politicians were like the quarrels between the girls in a brothel – they would tear each other's hair one night, do a trick together the next. They had no memory. They had no principles but for one – you do not quit the house. You may kill each other but you do not quit the house.

One could imagine the end of an imaginary nightmare: some time in the future, the Iron Ham (for such had become the fond nickname attached to President Barry Goldwater) would be told, thinking back on it all, that Billy-boy Scranton should be removed for some of the things he had said, and old Eisenhower, our General Emeritus, would find it in himself to say at a Press Conference on TV that while removal could not in itself be condoned, that is for high political figures, still it was bad, of course, policy, for people to have gotten away with insulting the President even if it was in the past and in the guise of free speech which as we all know can be abused. They would shave Scranton's head. Like a monk would he take the walk. And Old Ike would walk with him, and tell Willy S. a joke at the end, and have his picture taken shaking hands. Then, back to the White House for a two-shot drinking beer with Barry, the Iron Ham. After it was over Barry would go back to the people who had put the ring in his nose.

. . . They should not think it amongst their rights to cut off the entail, or commit waste on the inheritance, by destroying at

their pleasure the whole original fabric of their society; haz-
arding to leave to those who come after them a ruin instead of a
habitation.

　　　　　　　　　– BURKE, *Reflections on the Revolution in France*

Goldwater: 'There have been several suggestions made. I don't
think we would use any of them. But defoliation of the forests
by low-yield atomic weapons could well be done. When you
remove the foliage, you remove the cover.'

　　　　　　　　　　　　　– *New York Post*, May 27, 1964

Driving away from the Cow Palace after the nomination, I
could hear Goldwater on the car radio. He was celebrating.
He was considerably more agreeable than Dick Nixon cele-
brating – no all-I-am-I-owe-to-my-mother-and-father-my-
country-and-church; no, Goldwater was off instead on one
of his mild rather tangy excursions, 'I feel very humble,' he
said, and you could feel the itch in the long johns and the
hair in the nose, a traveling salesman in an upper berth, belt
of bourbon down the hatch – as Mrs Goldwater entered the
room, he cried out, 'Hi, honey,' and added just a touch mean
and small-town, 'You didn't cry very much tonight.'

'No,' said Mrs Goldwater, 'Wait till tomorrow.'

The questioning went back and forth. He was all voice
and very little mind, you could tell he had once been so
bright as to invent and market a novelty item called Antsy
Pants, men's white shorts with red ants embroidered all over
them. But he had a voice! It made up for the mind. Lyndon
Johnson's hambone-grits-and-turnip-greens was going to
play heavy to this; Goldwater on radio was sweet and
manly, clean as Dad in the show of new shows, One Man's
Dad. They asked him, *Senator, you said that you would not*
wage a personal campaign against the President. 'Yes,' said
Goldwater. *Well, sir,* said the interviewer now, *today you*
called President Johnson the biggest faker in the U.S.
Butters of ecstasy in the interviewer's mouth. *It's going to be*
a hard-hitting campaign, I assume then? 'Oh,' said Gold-

water, 'I think you'll find some brickbats flying around.'

The dialogue went on: *Could you tick off just a few of the major issues you think will be in the campaign against the Democrats?* 'I think,' said Goldwater, 'law and dis – the abuse of law and order in this country, the total disregard for it, the mounting crime rate is going to be another issue – at least I'm going to make it one, because I think the responsibility for this has to start someplace and it should start at the Federal level with the Federal courts enforcing the law.

'I noticed one tonight in the evening paper, for example – a young girl in New York who used a knife to attack a rapist is now getting the worst of the deal and the rapist is probably going to get the Congressional Medal of Honor and sent off scot-free,' said Goldwater, neglecting to tell us that the girl had had her indictment dismissed, and the alleged rapist was already up on a charge of attempted rape. Goldwater now said in the sort of voice Daddy employs when he is ready to use the strap, 'That kind of business has to stop in this country and, as the President, I'm going to do all I can to see that women can go out in the streets of this country without being scared stiff.' Yes, he would. He was a Conservative and he was for States' Rights. It was just that he wasn't for *local* rights.

'By this wise prejudice we are taught to look with horror on those children of their country, who are prompt rashly to hack that aged parent in pieces, and put him into the kettle of magicians, in hopes that by their poisonous weeds, and wild incantations, they may regenerate the paternal constitution, and renovate their father's life.'

— BURKE, *Reflections on the Revolution in France*

Next day was the last day of the convention. Bill Miller was nominated for Vice-President. He was not a very handsome man nor did his manner seem particularly agreeable, but then the thought obtruded itself that the President of the United States was now in a more dramatic statistical relation to violent death than a matador. So a candidate would not necessarily look for too appealing a Vice-President – it might encourage notions of succession in the mind of an assassin. One would look instead for deterrents. William Miller was a deterrent.

III

A little later on the last day, Nixon made the speech of introduction for Goldwater. In the months ahead, when the bull in Barry swelled too wild and he gave promise of talking again of Negro assailants getting Medals of Honor, they would send in Nixon to calm him down. The Eastern Establishment, hydra head, was not dead after all; they still had Nixon. He was the steer to soothe the bull. Poor Barry. He had tried to lose Nixon in Cleveland, he had said, 'He's sounding more like Harold Stassen every day.' Nixon however was as easy to lose as a plain wife without prospects is easy to divorce.

'My good friend and great Republican, Dick Nixon . . .' was how Goldwater began his historic acceptance speech. It had come after a rich demonstration of happiness from the delegates. A boxcar of small balloons was opened in the rafters as Goldwater came down the ramp with his wife, his sons, his daughters. The balloons tumbled in thousands to the floor where (fifty balloons being put out each second by lighted cigarettes) a sound like machine-gun fire popped its way through the cheers. Fourth of July was here once more. He looked good, did Goldwater. Looking up at him from a position just beneath the speaker's stand, not twenty feet away, it was undeniable that Barry looked as handsome as a man who had just won the five-hundred-mile race in Indianapolis, had gone home to dress, and was now attending a party in his honor. He was even, protect the mark, elegant.

Then he began his speech. Today, the voice for large public gatherings had dignity. It was not a great voice, as Churchill's voice was great; there were no majesties nor storms of complexity, no war of style between manner and the obligation to say truth; but it was a balanced manly voice which would get votes. His speech was good in its beginning.

> *Now my fellow Americans, the tide has been running against freedom. Our people have followed false prophets ... We must, and we shall, set the tide running again in the cause of freedom ... Every breath and every heartbeat has but a single resolve, and that is freedom ... Tonight there is violence in our streets, corruption in our highest offices, aimlessness among our youth, anxiety among our elderly ... despair among the many who look beyond material success toward the inner meaning of their lives.*

As the speech went on, the mind went out again on a calculation that this candidate could win. He was humbug – H. L. Hunt's idea of freedom would not be very close to the idea of freedom in the minds of the children who were for Barry, no, nor William Knowland's idea either, no, nor the Pinkertons, the hawkshaw *geist* of the F.B.I., nor the four-teenth and fifteenth floor. Goldwater was a demagogue – he permitted his supporters to sell a drink called Gold Water, twenty-five cents a can for orange concentrate and warm soda – let no one say it went down like piss – he was a demagogue. He was also sincere. That was the damnable difficulty. Half-Jew and blue-eyed – if you belonged in the breed, you knew it was manic-depressive for sure: a man who designed his own electronic flagpole to raise Old Glory at dawn, pull her down at dusk – he had an instinct for the heart of the disease – he knew how to bring balm to the mad, or at least to half the mad; Goldwater would have much to learn about Negroes. But one thing was certain: he could win. He would be breadwinner, husband and rogue to the underprivileged of the psyche, he would strike a spark in many dry souls for he offered release to frustrations deeper than politics. Therefore, he could beat Lyndon Johnson, he could beat him out of a variety of cause, out of natural flood or hurricane, in an epidemic of backlash, or by an epidemic of guilt – how many union workers fed to the nose with exhortations that Johnson was good for take-home pay might rise and say to themselves, 'I've been happy with less.' Indeed I knew Goldwater could win because something in me leaped at the thought; a part of me, a devil, wished to take that choice. For if Goldwater were President, a new opposition would form, an underground – the time for secret armies might be near again. And when in sanity I thought, Lord, give us twenty more years of Lyndon Johnson, nausea rose in some cellar of the throat, my stomach was not strong enough to bear such security; and if true for me, true for others, true perhaps for half or more of a nation's vote. Yet what of totalitarianism? What of war? But what of war? And the answer came back that one might be better a little nearer to death than the soul dying each night in the plastic encirclements of the new architecture and the new city, yes better, if death had dimension and one could know the face of the enemy and leave a curse. What blessing to know the face of the enemy by the end of the second third of the twentieth century.

And what of the Negro if Goldwater won? What of all the small-town Southern sheriffs who wished to wipe their hands in the black man's hair? And a fury, a white fury, burst out of the mind and said, 'No white sheriff is necessarily so very much worse than the worst Negro,' no, the mad light of the black hoodlum might be getting equal geek to geek to the worst of the California delegation. Then came a memory of James Baldwin and Diana Sands on a show called *Night Line* where television viewers could make a telephone call to the guests. Baldwin had received a call from a liberal which went, 'I'd like to help, and I'm asking you how.' 'Don't ask me, baby,' said Baldwin, 'ask yourself.'

'You don't understand,' said the liberal, 'I know something about these matters, but it's getting confusing for me. I'm asking you in all sincerity where you think my help could be best offered.' 'Well, baby,' said Baldwin, 'that's *your* problem.' And Diana Sands, pinky extended in total delicate black-lady disgust, put the receiver back in the cradle. 'You see,' said Baldwin, talking to Les Crane, the master of ceremonies, 'I remember what an old Negro woman told me once down South. She said, "What the white man will someday learn is that there is no remission of sin." That I never forgot,' said Jimmy, 'because you see it's perfectly possible the white will not be forgiven, not for a single cut or whipping or lynch mob or rape of a black woman,' his voice now as soft and reminiscent of the wind as some African man of witchcraft. And I had to throttle an impulse to pick up the phone and call Baldwin, and say, 'You get *this*, baby. There's a shit storm coming like nothing you ever knew. So ask yourself if what you desire is for the white to kill every black so that there be total remission of guilt in your black soul.' And the mind went out still again.

The country was in disease, it was conceivably so ill that a butcher could operate with dirty hands and have magic sufficient to do less harm than the hospital with its wonder drugs and the new pestilence. (As the oil goes out, the earth turns cold, an arid used-up space, a ground for jumping off Texas to the used-up pits of the moon.) Still, you could not keep Americans from madness; our poetry was there, our symbolic logic: $AuH_2O + GOP + 64 = Victory!$ color of orange juice, Go, Go, Goldwater. Mrs Goldwater's maiden name was Johnson, a portent of triumph to Barry? *Viva-Olé*. Eager to slay.

The country was in disease. It had been in disease for a long time. There was nothing in our growth which was organic. We had never solved our depression, we had merely gone to war, and going to war had never won it, not in our own minds, not as men, no, we had won it but as mothers, sources of supply; we did not know that we were equal to the Russians. We had won a war but we had not really won it, not in the secret of our sleep. So we had not really had a prosperity, we had had fever. *Viva-Olé.* We had grown rich because of one fact with two opposite interpretations: there had been a cold war. It was a cold war which had come because Communism was indeed a real threat to freedom, or it had come because capitalism would never survive without an economy geared to war; or was it both – who could know? who could really know? The center of our motive was the riddle wrapped in the enigma – was the country extraordinary or accursed? No, we had not even found our Communist threat. We had had a secret police organization and an invisible government large enough by now to occupy the moon, we had hunted Communists from the top of the Time-Life Building to the bottom of the Collier mine; we had not found that many, not that many, and had looked like Keystone cops. We had even had a Negro Revolution in which we did not believe. We had had it, yes we had had it, because (in the penury of our motive) we could not afford to lose votes in Africa and India, South America and Japan, Vietnam, the Philippines, name any impoverished place: we were running in a world election against the collective image of the Russ, and so we had to give the black man his civil rights or Africa was so much nearer to Marx. But there had not been much like love in the civil rights. Just Dirksen. So we were never too authentic. No.

We had had a hero. He was a young good-looking man with a beautiful wife, and he had won the biggest poker game we ever played, the only real one – we had lived for a week ready to die in a nuclear war. Whether we liked it or not. But he had won. It was our one true victory in all these years, our moment; so the young man began to inspire a subtle kind of love. His strength had proved stronger than we knew. Suddenly he was dead, and we were in grief. But then came a trial which was worse. For the assassin, or the man who had been arrested but was not the assassin – we would never know, not really – was killed before our sight.

In the middle of the funeral came an explosion on the porch.
Now, we were going mad. It took more to make a nation go
mad than any separate man, but we had taken miles too
much. Certainties had shattered. Now the voice of our
national nerves (our arts, our events) was in a new state.
Morality had wed itself to surrealism, there were cock-
roaches in all the purple transistors, we were distractable.
We had an art of the absurd; we had moral surrealism. Our
best art was *Dr Strangelove* and *Naked Lunch, Catch-22;*
Candy was our heroine; Jack Ruby our aging juvenile;
Andy Warhol, Rembrandt; our national love was a corpse
in Arlington; and heavyweight champion turned out to be
Cassius Clay; New York was the World's Fair plus the
Harlem bomb – it would take a genius to explain they were
the same – and Jimmy Baldwin said, 'That's *your* problem,'
on the Les Crane show at one a.m. Even the reverends were
salty as the sea.

Yes, our country was fearful, half mad, inauthentic. It
needed a purge. It had a liberal Establishment obeisant to
committees, foundations, and science – the liberal did not
understand that the center of science was as nihilistic as a
psychopath's sense of God. We were a liberal Establish-
ment, a prosperous land – we had a Roman consul among us
– the much underrated and much disliked Lyndon Johnson
was become a power in the land and doubtless a power upon
the land; civilization had found its newest helmsman in the
restraints, wisdom, and corruption of a major politician, of
an organization boss to whom all Mafias, legit and illegit, all
syndicates, unions, guilds, corporations and institutions,
cadres of conspiracy and agents for health, Medicare, wel-
fare, the preservation of antibiotics, and the proliferation of
the Pentagon could bend their knee. The Establishment (the
Democratic Establishment and the reeling columns of the
Republican Establishment, falling back upon the center in
the thundering confusion of Barry Goldwater's break-
through) had a new leader, a mighty Caesar had arisen,
Lyndon Johnson was his name, all hail, Caesar. Caesar gave

promise to unify the land. But at what a cost. For if the ideology were liberal, the methodology was total – to this political church would come Adlai Stevenson and Frank Sinatra, the President of U.S. Steel and the President of the Steel Workers' Union, there would be photographs of Johnson forty feet high in Atlantic City – Big Bubber Lyndon – and parties in which minority groups in native costume would have their folk dance: could one see the ghost of Joe Stalin smiling on his pipe?

Yes, if we all worked to beat Barry, and got behind Lyndon and pushed, radicals and moderate Republicans, Negroes and Southern liberals, college professors and Cosa Nostra, café society and Beatniks-for-Johnson, were we all then going down a liberal superhighway into the deepest swamp of them all? For Johnson was intelligent enough to run a total land, he had vast competence, no vision, and the heart to hold huge power, he had the vanity of a Renaissance prince or a modern dictator, whereas Barry might secretly be happier with his own show daily on radio. If Goldwater were elected, he could not control the country without moving to the center; moving to the center he would lose a part of the Right, satisfy no one, and be obliged to drift still further Left, or moving back to the Right would open schisms across the land which could not be closed. Goldwater elected, America would stand revealed, its latent treacheries would pop forth like boils; Johnson elected, the drift would go on, the San Francisco Hiltons would deploy among us. Under Goldwater, the odds were certainly greater that nuclear war would come, but under Johnson we could move from the threat of total war to war itself with nothing to prevent it; the anti-Goldwater forces which might keep the country too divided to go to war would now be contained within Johnson. Goldwater promised to lead the nation across the edge of a precipice, Johnson would walk us through the woods, perchance to quicksand itself. Goldwater would open us to the perils of our madness, Johnson would continue our trip into the plague. Goldwater could accelerate the Negro Revolution to violence and disaster – Johnson might yet be obliged to betray it from within. And what a job could be done! Who in such a pass should receive the blessing of a vote – the man who inspired the deepest fear, or the man who encouraged us to live in a lard of guilt cold as the most mediocre of our satisfied needs?

Still, the more Goldwater talked, the less impressive became his voice. When he went on too long, his voice grew barren. One could never vote for him, one could not vote for a man who made a career by crying Communist – that was too easy: half the pigs, bullies, and cowards of the twentieth century had made their fortune on that fear. I had a moment of rage at the swindle. I was tired of hearing about Barry Goldwater's high fine courage. Yesterday, on the floor, talking to a young delegate from Indiana, I had said, 'Did it ever occur to you that Fidel Castro might have more courage than Barry Goldwater?'

'Yes, but Castro is a criminal mentality,' said the boy.

I had cut off the argument. I was too close to losing my temper. Would the best of the young in every hick town, washed by the brainwater of the high school and the Legion, come to join this conservative crusade because Goldwater made an appeal to freedom, to courage, to change? What a swindle was in the making, what an extinction of the best in Conservative thought. They were so righteous, these Republicans. Goldwater might end with more warfare, security, and statism than any Democrat had ever dared; as a conservative, he would fail altogether (doubtless!) but certain he was to do one thing: he would march into Cuba. That was too much. One could live with a country which was mad, one could even come to love her (for there was agony beneath the madness), but you could not share your life with a nation which was powerful, a coward, and righteously pleased because a foe one-hundredth our size had been destroyed. So one got up to leave at this – we would certainly be strong enough to march into Cuba.

Then Goldwater uttered his most historic words:

'Extremism in the defense of liberty is no vice . . . Moderation in the pursuit of justice is no virtue,' and I sat down and took out my notebook and wrote in his words, since I did not know how famous they would become. And thought: Dad, you're too much. You're really too much. You're too hip, baby. I have spent my life seeking to get four-letter words into U.S. magazines, and now you are ready to help me.

And as I left the arena, there was a fire engine and the cry of a siren and the police with a gaunt grim look for the end of the week. There had been a fire burning, some small fire.

On the way out, outside the Cow Palace, a wet fog was drifting, and out beyond the exits, demonstrators from CORE were making a march. They had been out there every day of the convention: Monday, Tuesday, Wednesday, and Thursday now, each day had demonstrated, carrying their placards, marching in a circle two abreast, singing *We Shall Overcome*, shouting, 'Goldwater Must Go', marching round and round like early Christians in the corrals waiting to be sent to the arena, while about them, five, six, ten deep, was a crowd of the Republican curious, some with troubled faces, some with faces troubled by no more than appetite, hounds staring at the meat, these white girls and Negro boys walking side by side, the girls pale, no lipstick, nunlike, disdainful, wearing denim shirts and dungarees; the Negroes tall and sometimes handsome, not without dignity, bearded almost all, the wild Negro girl in the center screaming savage taunts at the watching crowd, rude as Cassius Clay with a high-yaller mouth, and the crowd dreaming of an arena where lions could be set on these cohabiting blacks and whites, and the blacks and whites in the marching circle with their disdainful faces. Yes, kill us, says the expression on the face of the nunlike girl with no lipstick, you will kill us but you will never digest us: I despise you all. And some of the old Wasps are troubled in their Christian hearts for the girl is one of theirs, no fat plain Jewess with a poor nose is this one, she is part of the West, and so their sense of crisis opens and they know like me that America has come to a point from which she will never return. The wars are coming and the deep revolutions of the soul.

Our Argument Picturesquely Continued

One extraordinary error in the last piece. It assumed Gold-
water would do well. He proved too dogged, however, to be
a demagogue, and his campaign was singularly inept – the
real possibility of what he had to offer America would not
appear until Vietnam. In the meantime, one had been to the
Democratic Convention. It took place in Atlantic City,
which is perhaps the filthiest city in America, its window
sills as greasy as its alleys, over a stretch of sultry days which
spoke of future hurricane, and Hubert Humphrey was the
symbol, appearing everywhere, smiling, smiling with the
used-up, spirit-sucked face of an actor who has been smiling
for twenty years.

The Mafia was there on the fringe, minor-league Mafia,
with beehive head-dresses on the hustlers from Newark, and
small-beer hoods, and the Democratic Establishment every-
where, blank, blank as the smile in a dull woman's eye. And
Lyndon Johnson's two pictures flank and flank to the
podium, two pictures going forty feet up. On the floor were
factions. They had little to do with one another. They were
too far apart in their beginnings, C.I.O. and Southern
manse, but they were gotten together for the convention,
and between speeches there was as much enthusiasm on the
floor of Convention Hall as can be found in a large railroad
station on a summer afternoon.

PART TWO: LIONS

The Argument Reinvigorated

Reader, a telegram: SHIFT MCNAMARA LAMBS FROM WARS OF JELLIED FIRE TO LIONS IN BURNING BUSH.

Assume I am a lecturer in the fields of Fellowship surrounding Literature (American) and am trying to draw some grand design in twenty minutes on a talk devoted to 'The Dynamic of American Letters'. Knowing attention is iron for the blood of a Fellow, I will not be so foolish as to perish without a look at the topical and the interesting. No, I will use 'The Dynamic of American Letters' as preparation for a lightning discussion of Herzog and Terry Southern, with a coda on the art of the absurd. Let me then have my first sentence as lecturer: 'There has been a war at the center of American letters for a long time.' That is not so poor. The look of absolute comprehension on the face of the audience encourages the lecturer to go on.

The war began as a class war; an upper-middle class looked for a development of its taste, a definition of its manners, a refinement of itself to prepare a shift to the aristocratic; that was its private demand upon culture. That demand is still being made by a magazine called The New Yorker. *This upper-class development of literature was invaded a long time ago, however, back at the cusp of the century, by a counter-literature whose roots were found in poverty, industrial society, and the emergence of new class. It was a literature which grappled with a peculiarly American phenomenon – a tendency of American society to alter more rapidly than the ability of its artists to record that change. Now, of course, one might go back two thousand years into China to find a society which did not alter more rapidly than its culture, but the American phenomenon had to do with the very rate of acceleration. The order of magnitude in this rate had shifted. It was as if everything changed ten times as fast in America, and this made for extraordinary difficulty in creating a literature. The sound, sensible, morally stout delineation of society which one found in Tolstoy and Balzac and Zola, in Thackeray and in Trollope, had become impossible. The American novelist of manners had to content himself with manners – he could not put a convincing servant into his work, and certainly not a workingman, because they were moving themselves in one generation out from the pantry into the morning dress of the lady in the parlor and up from the foundry to the master of the factory. The novelist of manners could not go near these matters – they promised to take over all of his book. So the job was left to Howells, Stephen Crane, to Dreiser, and in lesser degree to such writers as Norris, Jack London, Upton Sinclair – let us say it was left to Dreiser. A fundamental irony of American letters had not presented itself. For in opposition to Dreiser was the imperfectly developed countertradition of the genteel. The class which wielded the power which ran America, and the class which most admired that class, banded instinctively together to approve a genteel literature which had little to do with power or the secrets of power. They encouraged a literature about court- ship and marriage and love and play and devotion and piety and style, a literature which had to do finally with the excel- lence of belonging to their own genteel tradition. Thus it was a literature which borrowed the forms of its conduct from European models. The people who were most American by birth, and who had the most to do with managing America, gave themselves a literature which had the least to say about the real phenomena of American life, most particularly the accelerated rate, the awful rate, of growth and anomaly through all of society. That sort of literature and that kind of attempt to explain America was left to the sons of immi- grants who, if they were vigorous enough, and fortunate enough to be educated, now had the opportunity to see that*

America was a phenomenon never before described, indeed never before visible in the record of history. There was something going on in American life which was either grand or horrible or both, but it was going on – at a dizzy rate – and the future glory or doom of the world was not necessarily divorced from it. Dreiser labored like a titan to capture the phenomenon; he became a titan; Thomas Wolfe, his only peer as giant (as the novelist-as-giant), labored also like a titan, but for half as long and died in terror of the gargantuan proportions of the task. Yet each failed in one part of the job. They were able to describe society – Wolfe like the greatest five-year-old who ever lived,* an invaluable achievement, and Dreiser like some heroic tragic entrepreneur who has reasoned out through his own fatigue and travail very much how everything works in the iron mills of life, but is damned because he cannot pass on the knowledge to his children. Dreiser and Wolfe were up from the people, and Dreiser particularly came closer to understanding the social machine than any American writer who ever lived, but he paid an unendurable price – he was forced to alienate himself from manner in order to learn the vast amount he learned. Manner insists one learn at a modest rate, that one learn each step with grace before going on to the next. Dreiser was in a huge hurry, he had to learn everything – that was the way he must have felt his mission, so there is nothing of manner in his work; which is to say, nothing of tactics.

If the upper-class quite naturally likes a literature which is good for them, a literature at the surface perhaps trivial, but underneath amusing, elucidative, fortifying, *it is because this kind of literature elaborates and clarifies the details of their life, and thus adjusts their sense of power, their upper-class*

* This Argument was delivered, originally, as a talk to The American Studies Association and the M.L.A. This remark brought laughter from the audience. Since I did not wish to insult the memory of Wolfe, it would have been happier and perhaps more accurate to have said: like the greatest fifteen-year-old alive.

sense of power, which is invariably lubricated by a sense of detail. So too does that other class of readers in American literature, that huge, loose, all but unassociated congregation of readers – immigrant, proletarian, entrepreneur – wish in turn for a literature which is equally good for them. That is where Dreiser had to fail. He was only half-good for such readers. He taught them strategy as Americans had never gotten it before in a novel. If they were adventurers, he was almost as useful to them as Stendhal was exceptionally useful to a century of French intellectuals who had come to Paris from the provinces. But not quite. Dreiser, finally, is not quite as useful, and the difference is crucial. Because a young adventurer reads a great novel in the unvoiced hope it is a grindstone which sharpens his axe sufficiently to smash down doors now locked to him. Dreiser merely located the doors and gave warnings about the secret padlocks and the traps. But he had no grindstone, no manner, no eye for the deadly important manners of the rich, he was obliged to call a rich girl 'charming'; he could not make her charming when she spoke, as Fitzgerald could, and so he did not really prepare the army of his readers for what was ahead. His task was doubly difficult – it was required of him to give every upstart fresh strategy and tactics. No less than the secret sociology of society is what is needed by the upstart and that strategy Dreiser gave him. But tactics – the manners of the drawing room, the deaths and lifes of the drawing room, the cocktail party, the glorious tactics of the individual kill – that was all beyond him. Dreiser went blind climbing the mountains of society, so he could not help anyone to see what was directly before him – only what had happened and what was likely to come next.

That was the initial shape of the war, Naturalism versus the Genteel Tradition it has been called, and one might pose Henry James against Dreiser, but James is sufficiently great a writer to violate the generalizations one must make about the novel of manners which must always – precisely because it deals with manners – eschew the overambitious, plus ex-

tremes of plot – which James of course did not. So let us say the war was between Dreiser and Edith Wharton, Dreiser all strategy, no tactics; and Wharton all tactics. Marvelous tactics they were – a jewel of a writer and stingy as a parson – she needed no strategy. The upper-class writer had all strategy provided him by the logic of his class. Maybe that is why the war never came to decision, or even to conclusion. No upper-class writer went down into the pits to bring back the manner alive of the change going on down there, *certainly not Edith Wharton, not James Branch Cabell, of course not, nor Hergesheimer nor even Cather or Glasgow, not Elinor Wylie, no, nor Carl Van Vechten, and no diamond in the rough was ever reshaped by the cutters of Newport. The gap in American letters continued. Upper-class writers like John Dos Passos made brave efforts to go down and get the stuff and never quite got it, mainly in Dos Passos's case because they lacked strategy for the depths – manners may be sufficient to delineate the rich but one needs a vision of society to comprehend the poor, and Dos Passos had only revulsion at injustice, which is ultimately a manner. Some upper-class writers like Fitzgerald turned delicately upon the suppositions of their class, lost all borrowed strategy and were rudderless, were forced therefore to become superb in tactics, but for this reason perhaps a kind of hysteria lived at the center of their work; lower-class writers like Farrell and Steinbeck described whole seas of the uncharted ocean but their characters did not push from one milieu into another, and so the results were more taxonomic than apocalyptic.*

Since then the war has shifted. No writer succeeded in doing the single great work which would clarify a nation's vision of itself as Tolstoy had done perhaps with War and Peace *or* Anna Karenina, *and Stendhal with* The Red and the Black, *no one novel came along which was grand and daring and comprehensive and detailed, able to give sustenance to the adventurer and merriment to the rich, leave compassion in the icechambers of the upper class and energy as alms for the poor. (Not unless it was* Tropic of Cancer.) *Dreiser came as close as any, and never got close at all, for he could not capture the moment, and no country in history has lived perhaps so much for the moment as America. After his heroic failure, American literature was isolated – it was necessary to give courses in American literature to Americans, either because they would not otherwise read it, or because reading it, they could not understand it. It was not quite vital to them. It did not save their lives, make them more ambitious, more moral, more tormented, more audacious, more ready for love, more ready for war, for charity and for invention. No, it tended to puzzle them. The realistic literature had never caught up with the rate of change in American life, indeed it had fallen further and further behind, and the novel gave up any desire to be a creation equal to the phenomenon of the country itself; it settled for being a metaphor. Which is to say that each separate author made a separate peace. He would no longer try to capture America, he would merely try to give life to some microcosm in American life, some metaphor – in the sense that a drop of water is a metaphor of the seas, or a hair of the beast is for some a metaphor of the beast – and in that metaphor he might – if he were very lucky – have it all, rich and poor, strategy and tactics, insight and manner, detail, authority, the works. He would have it all for a particular few. It was just that he was no longer writing about the beast but, as in the case of Hemingway (if we are to take the best of this), about the paw of the beast, or in Faulkner about the dreams of the beast. What a paw and what dreams! Perhaps they are the two greatest writers America ever had, but they had given up on trying to do it all. Their vision was partial, determinedly so, they saw that as the first condition for trying to be great – that one must not try to save. Not souls, and not the nation. The desire for majesty was the bitch which licked at the literary loins of Hemingway and Faulkner: the country could be damned. Let it take care of itself.*

*And of course the country did. Just that. It grew by itself.
Like a weed and a monster and a beauty and a pig. And the
task of explaining America was taken over by Luce maga-
zines. Those few aristocratic novelistic sensibilities which
had never seen the task of defining the country as one for
them – it was finally most unamusing as a task – grew
smaller and smaller and more and more superb. Edith
Wharton reappeared as Truman Capote, even more of a
jewel, even stingier. Of writers up from the bottom there
were numbers: Dreiser's nephews were as far apart as Saul
Bellow and James Jones. But the difference between the two
kinds of writers had shifted. It had begun to shift some-
where after the Second World War, and the shift had gone
a distance. One could not speak at all now of aristocratic
writers and novelists whose work was itself the protagonist
to carry the writer and his readers through the locks of
society; no, the work had long since retreated, the great am-
bition was gone, and then it was worse, even the metaphor
was gone, the paw of the beast and the dreams of the beast,
no, literature was down to the earnest novel and the perfect
novel, to moral seriousness and Camp. Herzog and Candy
had become the protagonists.*

*Frank Cowperwood once amassed an empire. Herzog, his
bastard great-nephew, diddled in the ruins of an intellectual
warehouse. Where once the realistic novel cut a swath across
the face of society, now its reality was concentrated into
moral seriousness. Where the original heroes of naturalism
had been active, bold, self-centered, close to tragic, and up
to their nostrils in their exertions to advance their own life
and force the webs of society, so the hero of moral earn-
estness, the hero Herzog and the hero Levin in Malamud's
A New Life, are men who represent the contrary – passive,
timid, other-directed, pathetic, up to the nostrils in anguish:
the world is stronger than they are; suicide calls.*

*Malamud's hero is more active than Herzog, he is also
more likeable, but these positive qualities keep the case from
being so pure. There is a mystery about the reception of*

Herzog. *For beneath its richness of texture and its wealth of
detail, the fact remains: never has a novel been so successful
when its hero was so dim. Not one of the critics who adored
the book would ever have permitted Herzog to remain an
hour in his house. For Herzog was defeated, Herzog was an
unoriginal man, Herzog was a fool – not an attractive God-
anointed fool like Gimpel the Fool, his direct progenitor,
but a sodden fool, over-educated and inept, unable to fight,
able to love only when love presented itself as a gift. Herzog
was intellectual but not bright, his ideas not original, his
style as it appeared in his letters unendurable – it had exactly
the leaden-footed sense of phrase which men laden with
anxiety and near to going mad put into their com-
munications. Herzog was hopeless. We learned nothing
about society from him, not even anything about his life.
And he is the only figure in the book. His wives, his mistress,
his family, his children, his friends, even the man who cuck-
olds him are seen on the periphery of a dimming vision.
Like all men near to being mad, his attention is within, but
the inner attention is without genius. Herzog is dull, he is
unendurably dull – he is like all those bright pedagogical
types who have a cavity at the center of their brain.*

*Yet the novel succeeds. There is its mystery. One reads it
with compassion. With rare compassion. Bored by Herzog,
still there is a secret burning of the heart. One's heart turns
over and produces a sorrow. Hardly any books are left to do
that.*

*Of course, Herzog is alive on sufferance. He is a beggar,
an extraordinary beggar who fixes you with his eye, his
breath, his clothing, his dank near-corrupt presence; he
haunts. Something goes on in Herzog's eye. It says: I am
debased, I am failed, I am near to rotten, and yet something
just as good and loving resides in me as the tenderest part of
your childhood. If the prophet Elijah sent me, it is not to
make you feel guilt but to weep. Suddenly, Herzog inspires
sorrow – touch of alchemy to the book – Herzog is at the
center of the modern dilemma. If we do not feel compassion*

for him, a forceful compassion which sends blood to warm
the limbs and the heart, then we are going to be forced to
shoot him. Because if Herzog does not arouse your com-
passion there is no other choice – he is too intolerable a
luxury to keep alive in his mediocrity unless he arouses your
love. The literary world chose to love him. We were not
ready to shoot Herzog. It all seemed too final if we did.
Because then there would be nothing left but Camp, and
Camp is the art of the Cannibal, Camp is the art which
evolved out of the bankruptcy of the novel of manners. It is
the partial thesis of these twenty minutes that the pure novel
of manners had watered down from The House of Mirth to
the maudlin middle reaches of The Rector of Justin; had in
fact gone all the way down the pike from The Ambassadors
to By Love Possessed. So, one does not speak of the novel of
manners any longer – one is obliged to look at the documen-
tary, In Cold Blood – or one is obliged to look at satire. The
aristocratic impulse turned upon itself produced one classic
– Terry Southern's The Magic Christian. Never had distaste
for the habits of a mass mob reached such precision, never
did wit falter in its natural assumption that the idiocies
of the mass were attached breath and kiss to the hypocrisies,
the weltering grandeurs, and the low stupidities of the rich,
the American rich. The aristocratic impulse to define society
by evocations of manner now survived only in the grace of
any cannibal sufficiently aristocratic to sup upon his own
family. The Magic Christian was a classic of Camp.

Note then: The two impulses in American letters had
failed, the realistic impulse never delivered the novel which
would ignite a nation's consciousness of itself, and the aristo-
cratic impulse clawed at the remaining fabric of a wealthy
society it despised and no longer wished to sustain. Like a
Tinguely machine which destroys itself, Camp amused by
the very act of its destruction. Since it was also sentimental,
the artifacts were necrophiliac.

Literature then had failed. The work was done by the
movies, by television. The consciousness of the masses and

the culture of the land trudged through endless mud.

The American consciousness in the absence of a great tradition in the novel ended by being developed by the boot-licking pieties of small-town newspaper editors and small-town educators, by the worst of organized religion, a form-less force filled with the terrors of all the Christians left to fill the spaces left by the initial bravery of the frontiersman, and these latterday Christians were simply not as brave. That was one component of the mud. The other was the sons of the immigrants. Many of them hated America, hated it for what it offered and did not provide, what it revealed of opportunity and what it excluded from real opportunity. The sons of these immigrants and the sons' sons took over the cities and began to run them, high up in the air and right down into the ground, they plucked and they plundered and there was not an American city which did not grow more hideous in the last fifty years. Then they spread out – they put suburbs like blight on the land – and piped mass com-munications into every home. They were cannibals selling Christianity to Christians, and because they despised the message and mocked at it in their own heart, they succeeded in selling something else, a virus perhaps, an electronic nihil-ism went through the mass media of America and entered the Christians and they were like to being cannibals, they were a tense and livid people, swallowing their own hate with the tranquilizers and the sex in the commercials, whereas all the early cannibals at the knobs of the mass-media made the mistake of passing on their bleak disease and were left now too gentle, too liberal, too programmatic, filled with plans for social welfare, and they looked and talked in Show Biz styles which possessed no style and were generally as unhealthy as Christians who lived in cellars and caves.

Yes, the cannibal sons of the immigrants had become Christians, and the formless form they had evolved for their mass-media, the hypocritical empty and tasteless taste of the television arts they beamed across the land encountered the formless form and the all but tasteless taste of the small-town tit-eating cannibal mind at its worst, and the collision produced schizophrenia in the land. Half of America went insane with head colds and medicaments and asthmas and allergies, hospitals and famous surgeons with knives to cut into the plague, welfares and plans and committees and co-operations and boredom, boredom plague deep upon the land; and the other part of America went ape, and the motorcycles began to roar like lions across the land and all the beasts of all the buried history of America turned in their circuit and prepared to slink toward the market place, there to burn the mother's hair and bite the baby to the heart. One thought of America and one thought of aspirin, kitchen-commercials, and blood. One thought of Vietnam. And the important art in America became the art of the absurd.

A good deal follows about the writing of contemporaries; there is criticism, some of it very critical. But then, good writing is not an act to excite tolerance because it is good, but anguish because it is not better. Who can swear there has not been something catastrophic to America in the failure of her novelists? Maybe we are the last liberators in the land, and if we continue to thrive on much less than our best, then the being of all of us may be deadened before we are done.
That is a statement which sups on the essence of extravagance, and yet it is the distance of the bridge to be built. It may be necessary that a communication of human experience, of the deepest and most unrecoverable human experience, must yet take place if we are to survive. Such at least is the covert opinion beneath the criticism which now follows.

Some Children of the Goddess

The last time I remember talking about the novel was a year ago, last June or July, and it was in a conversation with

Gore Vidal. We were reminiscing in mutually sour fashion over the various pirates, cutthroats, racketeers, assassins, pimps, rape artists, and general finks we had encountered on our separate travels through the literary world, and we went on at length, commenting – Gore with a certain bitter joy, I with some uneasiness – upon the decline of the novel in recent years. We were speaking as trade unionists. It was not that the American novel was necessarily less good than it had been immediately after the war, so much as that the people we knew seemed to care much less about novels. The working conditions were not as good. One rarely heard one's friends talking about a good new novel any more; it was always an essay in some magazine or a new play which seemed to occupy the five minutes in a dinner party when writers are discussed rather than politicians, friends, society or, elevate us, foreign affairs. One could not make one's living writing good novels any more. With an exception here and there, it had always been impossible, but not altogether – there had used to be the long chance of having a best seller. Now with paperback books, even a serious novel with extra-ordinarily good reviews was lucky to sell thirty thousand copies – most people preferred to wait a year and read the book later in its cheap edition.

So we went on about that, and the professional mediocrity of book reviewers and the indifference of publishers, the lack of community among novelists themselves, the back-biting, the glee with which most of us listened to unhappy news about other novelists, the general distaste of the occu-pation – its lonely hours, its jealous practitioners, its demands on one's character, its assaults on one's ego, its faithlessness as inspiration, its ambushes as fashion. Since we had both begun again to work on a novel after many years of working at every other kind of writing, there was a pleasant irony to all we said. We were not really as bitter as we sounded.

Finally, I laughed. 'Gore, admit it. The novel is like the Great Bitch in one's life. We think we're rid of her, we go on to other women, we take our pulse and decide that finally we're enjoying ourselves, we're free of her power, we'll never suffer her depredations again, and then we turn a corner on a street, and there's the Bitch smiling at us, and we're trapped. We're still trapped. We know the Bitch has still got us.'

Vidal gave that twisted grin of admiration which is extracted from him when someone else has coined an image which could fit his style. 'Indeed,' he said sighing, 'the novel *is* the Great Bitch.'

We've all had a piece of her, Nelson Algren, Jack Kerouac, myself, Ross Lockridge, Thomas Heggen, Truman Capote, John Horne Burns, Calder Willingham, Gore Vidal, Chandler Brossard, Walter van Tilburg Clark, Vance Bourjaily, William Humphrey, Willard Motley, Wright Morris, William Gaddis, Alex Trocchi – as well as the writers I'm going to talk about here, specifically James Jones, William Styron, Joseph Heller, John Updike, Philip Roth, Jimmy Baldwin, William Burroughs, Saul Bellow, J. D. Salinger – and all the writers there's not been time to read or write about this trip: James Purdy, Walker Percy, J. F. Powers, Ken Kesey, John Hawkes, Mark Harris, Louis Auchincloss, John Hersey, Clancy Sigal, J. P. Donleavy, Bernard Malamud, and how many others I've missed, and all the women, all the lady writers, bless them. But one cannot speak of a woman having a piece of the Bitch.

Let me list the novels I wish to discuss. They are *The Thin Red Line; Set This House on Fire; Naked Lunch; Catch-22; Rabbit, Run; Letting Go; Another Country; Henderson the Rain King; Franny and Zooey;* and *Raise High the Roof Beam, Carpenters.* They are not necessarily the best novels to have been written in America in the last few years, although if one could pick the best ten books of fiction which have been done in this country for the period, four or five of the titles on my list might have to be included. I chose these particular volumes by a particular test which might as well be explained.

It is impossible to read each good novel as it comes out. If you're trying to do your own work, it's distracting. Generally you stay away from the work of contemporaries for a year or two at a time: it saves a good deal of reading. It is amazing how many much-touted novels disappear in eighteen months. The underlying force in book reviewing is journalism. The editor of a book review has a section which he hopes to make as interesting to the owner of the newspaper as any other department. If, for two or three days, a newspaper is filled with news about a murder, one can be certain it is treated implicitly as the most exciting murder in the last twenty years. So with war novels, first novels, novels about homosexuality, politics, novels by authors of the Establishment, and historical novels. If I had a chapter of a novel for each review I've read of a new war novel which was said to be as good as *The Naked and the Dead* or *From Here to Eternity*, I would have fifty chapters. One never knows, of course. Maybe a few of these books are as good as they're said to be, and even if they've since disappeared, they will emerge again in ten or twenty years or in a century, but it is easier and much more logical to ignore what is said about a book when it first appears. There is too much direct and personal interest in the initial opinions, and much too much logrolling. The editor of a large book review is of course not owned by the Book-of-the-Month Club, but on the other hand the editor would just as soon not give more than two or three bad reviews in a year to book-club choices. Nor is his attitude dissimilar when it comes to choosing a reviewer for the novel which a big publishing house has chosen for its big book of the season. Robert Ruark, James Michener, Allen Drury will pick up their occasional roasts and slams, but considering how bad their books can be, it's impressive what attention they get. The slack (since a book review, depending on local tradition, can have just a certain proportion of good reviews) is taken up by misassigning small, determined literary types onto most of the really good novels, which then receive snide treatment and/or dismissal. *Catch-22*, for example, was reviewed on page fifty of *The New York Times Book Review*. Since this causes a vague uneasiness afterward in the book-review editor, there are always good young writers like Updike and Roth who get on the approved list and get many too many good reviews from bad reviewers. The point is that any serious novelist knows enough to stay out of the flurry which hits a new book. Every year whether the books deserve it or not, four or five first novelists will be provided a brilliant début and four or five respectable young novelists will receive the kind of review which 'enhances their reputation as one of the most serious and dedicated voices in the vineyard of literature.'

So you stay away. If your friends keep talking about certain books, and young writers, and girls at cocktail parties, if the talk is intriguing because as the months go by, you begin to have less and less of a clear impression of the books, then they come to install themselves on your reading list. And every year, or two years, or three, you go off on a binge for a month and gorge on the novels of your contemporaries and see how they made out on their night with the Bitch. But of course there are many books which you know are good and yet never get around to reading. For example, I had a lot of respect for *The Violated* by Vance Bourjaily. It gave me the feeling Bourjaily was capable of writing a major novel before he was through. His next book was *Confessions of a Spent Youth*. I dipped into it, and it seemed good to me, but it was good in the way of *The Violated*, it did not seem to go further. What I heard about it did not contradict my impression. So although Bourjaily was a friend, I never got around to reading *Confessions of a Spent Youth*. I still think that in ten years Bourjaily can be one of our four or five major novelists. He has great stamina and very decent insights which ride on a fine oil of humor, but the implicit logic of my method directed me away from Vance's last novel. It was not that I didn't think it would be good, but rather that I didn't think it would be different from what I expected. And when you're a professional and a gentleman gangster, your taste is for new weapons, not improvements on the old ones.

Now this emphasis upon the personal method of the critic may have justification. Trotsky once wrote that you can tell the truth by a comparison of the lies. Every novelist who has slept with the Bitch (only poets and writers of short stories have a *Muse*) comes away bragging afterward like a G.I. tumbling out of a whorehouse spree – 'Man, I made her moan,' goes the cry of the young writer. But the Bitch laughs afterward in her empty bed. 'He was so sweet in the beginning,' she declares, 'but by the end he just went, "Peep, peep, peep".' A man lays his character on the line when he writes a novel. Anything in him which is lazy, or meretricious, or unthought-out, or complacent, or fearful, or overambitious, or terrified by the ultimate logic of his exploration, will be revealed in his book. Some writers are skillful at concealing their weaknesses, some have a genius for converting a weakness into an acceptable mannerism of style. (One can even go so far as to say that Hemingway could never write a really good long sentence, and so cultivated the art of the short, whereas Faulkner could never express the simple very simply, and so flowered a great garden in the thicket of the non-stop prose.)

The notion is that a writer, no matter how great, is never altogether great; a small part of him remains a liar. Tolstoy evaded the depths which Dostoevsky opened; in turn Dostoevsky, lacking Tolstoy's majestic sense of the proportions of things, fled proportion and explored hysteria. A writer is recognized as great when his work is done, but while he is writing, he rarely feels so great. He is more likely to live with the anxiety of 'Can I do it? Should I let up here? Should I reconnoiter there? Will dread overwhelm me if I explore too far? or depression deaden me if I do not push on? Can I even do it?' As he writes, the writer is reshaping his character. He is a better man and he is worse, once he has finished a book. Potentialities in him have been developed, other talents have been sacrificed. He has made choices on his route and the choices have shaped him. By this understanding, a genius is a man of large talent who has made many good choices and a few astounding ones. He has had the wit to discipline his cowardice and he has had the courage to be bold where others might cry insanity. Yet no matter how large his genius, we can be certain of one thing – he could have been even greater. Dostoevsky was a very great writer, but if he had tried to be even greater he would either have cracked up or found impetus to write the *Confessions of a Great Sinner.* And if he had, the history of the world might have been different for it. It is even possible that Dostoevsky died in anguish, complimenting himself not at all for *The Brothers Karamazov* but hating himself for having so wasted a part of his talent that the greatest novel of them all was not written and he went with terror into death believing he had failed his Christ.

The example is extreme. Just so. There is a kind of critic who writes only about the dead. He sees the great writers of the past as simple men. They are born with a great talent, they exercise it, and they die. Such critics see the mastery in the work; they neglect the subtle failures of the most courageous intent, and the dramatic hours when the man took the leap to become a great writer. They do not understand that for every great writer, there are a hundred who could have been equally great but lacked the courage. For that reason it may be better to think of writers as pole vaulters than as artists. Pole vaulting is an act. The man who wins is the man who jumps the highest without knocking off the bar. And a man who clears the stick with precise form but eighteen inches below the record commands less of our attention. The writer, particularly the American writer, is not usually – if he is interesting – the quiet master of his craft; he is rather a being who ventures into the jungle of his unconscious to bring back a sense of order or a sense of chaos, he passes through ambushes in his sleep and, if he is ambitious, he must be ready to engage the congealed hostility of the world. If a writer is really good enough and bold enough he will, by the logic of society, write himself out onto the end of a limb which the world will saw off. He does not go necessarily to his death, but he must dare it. And some of us do go into death: Ross Lockridge, Thomas Heggen, Thomas Wolfe most especially, firing the passions which rotted his brain on those long paranoid nights in Brooklyn when he wrote in exaltation and terror on the top of a refrigerator. And Hemingway who dared death ten times over and would have had to dare it a hundred more in order to find more art, because each time he passed through death the sweet of new creativity was offered.

Well, few of us dare death. With the trinity of booze, coffee and cigarettes, most of us voyage out a part of the way into our jungle and come back filled with pride at what we dared, and shame at what we avoided, and because we are men of the middle and shame is an emotion no man of the middle can bear for too long without dying, we act like novelists, which is to say that we are full of spleen, small gossip, hatred for the success of our enemies, envy at the fortunes of our friends, ideologues of a style of fiction which is uniquely the best (and is invariably our own style), and so there is a tendency for us to approach the books of our contemporaries like a defense attorney walking up to a key witness for the prosecution. The average good novelist reads the work of his fellow racketeers with one underlying tension – find the flaw, find where the other guy cheated.

One cannot expect an objective performance therefore when one novelist criticizes the work of other novelists. It is better to realize that a group of men who are to a degree honest and to another extent deceitful (to the reader, or to themselves, or to both) are being judged by one of their peers who shares in the rough their proportions of integrity and pretense and is likely to have the most intense vested interest in advancing the reputation of certain writers while doing his best to diminish others. But the reader is at least given the opportunity to compare the lies, a gratuity he cannot always get from a good critic writing about a novelist, for critics implant into their style the fiction of disinterested passion when indeed *their* vested interest, while less obvious, is often more rabid, since they have usually fixed their aim into the direction they would like the novel to travel, whereas the novelist by the nature of his endeavor is more ready to change. One need not defend the procedure used here any further than to say it is preferable to warn a reader of one's prejudices than to believe the verdict of a review which is godly in its authority and psychologically unsigned.

I doubt if there is any book I read in the last few years which I approached with more unnatural passion than *Set This House on Fire*. Styron's first novel, *Lie Down in Darkness*, was published when he was twenty-six, and it was so good (one need today only compare it to *Rabbit, Run* to see how very good it was) that one felt a kind of awe about Styron. He gave promise of becoming a great writer, great not like Hemingway nor even like Faulkner, whom he resembled a bit, but great perhaps like Hawthorne. And there were minor echoes of Fitzgerald and Malcolm Lowry. Since his first novel had failed to make him a household word in America, he had a justifiable bitterness about the obscurity in which good young writers were kept. But it poisoned his reaction to everything. One of the traps for a writer of exceptional talent, recognized insufficiently, is the sort of excessive rage which washes out distinction. Styron was intensely competitive – all good young novelists are – but over the years envy began to eat into his character. Months before James Jones' *Some Came Running* was published (and it had the greatest advance publicity of any novel I remember – for publicity seemed to begin two years before publication), Styron obtained a copy of the galleys. There were long nights in Connecticut on 'Styron's Acres' when he would entertain a group of us by reading absurd passages from Jones' worst prose. I would laugh along with the rest, but I was a touch sick with myself. I had love for Jones, as well as an oversized fear for the breadth of his talent, and I had enough envy in me to enjoy how very bad were the worst parts of *Some Came Running*. But there were long powerful chapters as well; some of the best writing Jones has ever done is found in that book. So I would laugh in paroxysms along with the others, but I was also realizing that a part of me had wanted *Some Came Running* to be a major book. I was in the doldrums, I needed a charge of dynamite. If *Some Came Running* had turned out to be the best novel any of us had written since the war, I would have had to get to work. It would have meant the Bitch was in love with someone else, and I would have had to try to win her back. But the failure of *Some Came Running* left me holding onto a buttock of the lady – if she had many lovers, I was still one of them. And so everything in me which was slack and conservative could enjoy Styron's burlesque readings. Yet I also knew I had lost an opportunity.

A few months later, I ceased seeing Styron – it would take a chapter in a novel to tell you why. I liked the boy in Styron, disliked the man, and had vast admiration for his talent. I was hardly the one to read *Set This House on Fire* with a cool mind. Nine years had gone by since *Lie Down in Darkness* was published, and the anticipation of the second novel had taken on grandiloquent proportions among his friends and his closest enemies. One knew it would be close to unbearable if his book were extraordinary; yet a part of me felt again what I had known with *Some Came Running* – that it would be good for me and for my work if Styron's novel were better than anything any of us had done. So I read it with a hot sense of woe, delighted elation, and a fever of moral speculations. Because it was finally a bad novel. A bad maggoty novel. Four or five half-great short stories were buried like pullulating organs in a corpse of fecal matter, overblown unconceived philosophy, Technicolor melo-dramatics, and a staggering ignorance about the passions of murder, suicide and rape. It was the magnum opus of a fat

spoiled rich boy who could write like an angel about land-
scape and like an adolescent about people. The minor
characters were gargoyles, and badly drawn. Here and there
quick portraits emerged, there was one excellent still life of
an Italian police official who was Fascist, the set pieces were
laid out nicely, but the vice of the talent insisted on domi-
nating. Whenever Styron didn't know what to do with his
men and women (which was often, for they repeated them-
selves as endlessly as a Southern belle) Styron went back to
his landscape; more of the portentous Italian scenery blew
up its midnight storm. But Styron was trying to write a book
about good and evil, and his good was as vacuous as the
spirit of an empty water bag:

> *I can only tell you this, that as for being and nothing-*
> *ness, the one thing I did know was that to choose between*
> *them was simply to choose being, not for the sake of*
> *being, or even the love of being, much less the desire to be*
> *forever – but in the hope of being what I could be for a*
> *time.*

Which is a great help to all of us.
His evil character took on the fatal sin of an evil charac-
ter: he was not dangerous but pathetic. A fink. Styron was
crawling with all ten thumbs toward that ogre of mystery
who guards the secrets of why we choose to kill others and
quiver in dread at the urge to kill ourselves. But like a bad
general who surrounds himself with a staff which daren't
say no, Styron spent his time digging trenches for miles to
the left and miles to the right, and never launched an attack
on the hill before him. It was the book of a man whose soul
had gotten fat.
And yet, much as I could be superior to myself for having
taken him thus seriously, for having written predictions in
Advertisements for Myself that he would write a very good
book which the mass media would call great, much as I
would grin each day after reading a hundred pages of

hot-house beauty and butter bilge, much as I would think, 'You don't catch the Bitch that way, buster, you got to bring more than a trombone to her boudoir,' much so much as I was pleased at the moral justice which forbids a novelist who envied too much the life of others to capture much life in his own pages, I was still not altogether happy, because I knew his failure was making me complacent again, and so delaying once more the day when I would have to pay my respects to the lady.

And indeed I lost something by the failure of *Some Came Running* and *Set This House on Fire*. I never did get going far on my novel. I wrote a four-hour play and essays and articles, two hundred thousand words accumulated over the years since *Advertisements of Myself*, and I showed a talent for getting into stunts, and worse, much worse. Years went by. Now once again, in this season, ready to start my novel about the mysteries of murder and suicide,* I found by taking stock of psychic credit and debit that I had lost some of my competitive iron. I knew a bit of sadness about work. I did not feel sure I could do what I had now settled for doing, and to my surprise I was curious what others were up to. If I couldn't bring off the work by myself, it might be just as well if someone else could give a sign of being ready to make the attempt. In this sad dull mellow mood, feeling a little like a middle-aged mountaineer, I read at one stretch over three weeks the novels I want to write about here.

There was a time, I suspect, when James Jones wanted to be the greatest writer who ever lived. Now, if *The Thin Red Line* is evidence of his future, he has apparently decided to settle for being a very good writer among other good writers. The faults and barbarities of his style are gone. He is no longer the worst writer of prose ever to give intimations of greatness. The language has been filed down and the phrases

* This novel was a continuation thematically of the long novel announced in *Advertisements for Myself*. It was put aside six months later to go to work on *An American Dream*.

no longer collide like trailer trucks at a hot intersection. Yet I found myself nostalgic for the old bad prose. I never used to think it was as bad as others did, it was eloquent and communicated Jones' force to the reader. It is not that *The Thin Red Line* is dishonest or narrow; on the contrary it is so broad and true a portrait of combat that it could be used as a textbook at the Infantry School if the Army is any less chicken than it used to be. But, sign of the times, there is now something almost too workmanlike about Jones. He gets almost everything in, horror, fear, fatigue, the sport of combat, the hang-ups, details, tactics; he takes an infantry company through its early days in combat in Guadalcanal and quits it a few weeks later as a veteran outfit, blooded, tough, up on morale despite the loss of half the original men, gone, dead, wounded, sick or transferred. So he performs the virtuoso feat of letting us know a little about a hundred men. One can even (while reading) remember their names. Jones' aim, after all, is not to create character but the feel of combat, the psychology of men. He is close to a master at this. Jones has a strong sense of a man's psychology and it carries quietly through his pages.

The Thin Red Line was of course compared to *The Naked and the Dead*, but apart from the fact that I am the next-to-last man to judge the respective merits of the two books, I didn't see them as similar. *The Naked and the Dead* is concerned more with characters than military action. By comparison it's a leisurely performance. *The Thin Red Line* is as crammed as a movie treatment. No, I think the real comparison is to *The Red Badge of Courage*, and I suspect *The Red Badge of Courage* will outlive *The Thin Red Line*. Yet I don't quite know why. *The Thin Red Line* is a more detailed book; it tells much more of combat, studies the variations in courage and fear of not one man but twenty men and gets something good about each one of them. Its knowledge of life is superior to *The Red Badge of Courage*. *The Thin Red Line* is less sentimental, its humor is dry to the finest taste, and yet . . . it is too technical. One needs ten topographical maps to trace the action. With all its variety, scrupulosity, respect for craft, one doesn't remember *The Thin Red Line* with the same nostalgia, that same sense of a fire on the horizon which comes back always from *The Red Badge of Courage*.

No, Jones' book is better remembered as satisfying, as if one had studied geology for a semester and now knew more. I suppose what was felt lacking is the curious sensuousness of combat, the soft lift of awe and pleasure that one was moving out onto the rim of the dead. If one was not too tired, there were times when a blade of grass coming out of the ground before one's nose was as significant as the finger of Jehovah in the Sistine Chapel. And this was not because a blade of grass was necessarily in itself so beautiful, or because hitting the dirt was so sweet, but because the blade seemed to be a living part of the crack of small-arms fire and the palpable flotation of all the other souls in the platoon full of turd and glory. Now, it's not that Jones is altogether ignorant of this state. The description he uses is 'sexy', and one of the nicest things about Jim as a writer is his ease in moving from mystical to practical reactions with his characters. Few novelists can do this, it's the hint of greatness, but I think he steered *The Thin Red Line* away from its chance of becoming an American classic of the first rank when he kept the mystical side of his talents on bread and water, and gave his usual thoroughgoing company man's exhibition of how much he knows technically about his product. I think that is the mistake. War is as full of handbooks as engineering, but it is more of a mystery, and the mystery is what separates the great war novels from the good ones. It is an American activity to cover the ground quickly, but I guess this is one time Jones should have written two thousand pages, not four hundred ninety-five. But then the underlying passion in this book is not to go for broke, but to promise the vested idiots of the book reviews that he can write as good as anyone who writes a book review.

When you discuss eight or ten books, there is a dilemma. The choice is to write eight separate book reviews, or to work to find a thesis which ties the books together. There is something lickspittle about the second method: "Ten Authors in Search of a Viable Theme', or 'The Sense of Alienation in Eight American Novelists'. A bed of Procrustes is brought in from the wings to stretch and shorten the separate qualities of the books. I would rather pick up each book by itself and make my connections on the fly. The thesis of the Bitch is thesis enough for me. Its application to Jones would say that *The Thin Red Line* is a holding action, a long-distance call to the Goddess to declare that one still has one's hand in, expect red roses for sure, but for the time, you know, like there're contacts to make on the road, and a few Johns to impress.

Another Country, by James Baldwin, is as different from *The Thin Red Line* as two books by talented novelists published in the same year can turn out to be. It does not deal with a hundred characters, but eight, and they are very much related. In fact there is a chain of fornication which is all but complete. A Negro musician named Rufus Scott has an affair with a white Southern girl which ends in beatings, breakdown, and near-insanity. She goes to a mental hospital, he commits suicide. The connection is taken up by his sister who has an affair with a white writer, a friend of Rufus' named Vivaldo Moore, who in turn gets into bed with a friend named Eric who is homosexual but having an affair with a married woman named Cass Silenski, which affair wrecks her marriage with her husband, Richard, another writer, and leaves Eric waiting at the boat for his French lover Yves. A summary of this sort can do a book no good, but I make it to trace the links. With the exception of Rufus Scott, who does not go to bed with his sister, everybody else in the book is connected by their skin to another character who is connected to still another. So the principal in the book, the protagonist, is not an individual character, not society, not a milieu, not a social organism like an infantry company, but indeed is sex, sex very much in the act. And almost the only good writing in the book is about the act. And some of that is very good indeed. But *Another Country* is a shocker. For the most part it is an abominably written book. It is sluggish in its prose, lifeless for its first hundred pages, stilted to despair in its dialogue There are roles in plays called actor-proof. They are so conceived that even the worst actor will do fairly well. So *Another Country* is writer-proof. Its peculiar virtue is that Baldwin commits every *gaffe* in the art of novel writing and yet has a powerful book. It gets better of course; after the first hundred pages it gets a lot better. Once Eric, the homosexual, enters, the work picks up considerably. But what saves the scene is that Baldwin has gotten his hands into the meat and won't let go. All the sex in the book is displaced, whites with blacks, men with men, women with homosexuals; the sex is funky to suffocation, rich but claustrophobic, sensual, but airless. Baldwin understands the existential abyss of love. In a world of Negroes and whites, nuclear fallout, marijuana, bennies, inversion, insomnia, and tapering off with beer at four in the morning, one no longer just falls in love – one has to take a brave leap over the wall of one's impacted rage and cowardice. And nobody makes it, not quite. Each of the characters rides his sexual chariot, whip out, on a gallop over a solitary track, and each is smashed, more or less by his own hand. They cannot find the juice to break out of their hatred into the other country of love. Except for the homosexuals who can't break into heterosexual love. Of all the novels talked about here, *Another Country* is the one which is closest to the mood of New York in our time, a way of saying it is close to the air of the Western world, it is at least a novel about matters which are important, but one can't let up on Baldwin for the way he wrote it. Years ago I termed him 'minor' as a writer; I thought he was too smooth and too small. Now on his essays alone, on the long continuing line of poetic fire in his essays, one knows he has become one of the few writers of our time. But as a Negro novelist he could take lessons from a good journeyman like John Killens. Because *Another Country* is almost a major novel and yet it is far and away the weakest and worst near-major novel one has finished. It goes like the first draft of a first novelist who has such obvious stuff that one is ready, if an editor, to spend years guiding him into how to write, even as one winces at the sloppy company which must be kept. Nobody has more elegance than Baldwin as an essayist, not one of us hasn't learned something about the art of the essay from him, and yet he can't even find a good prose for his novel. Maybe the form is not for him. He knows what he wants to say, and that is not the best condition for writing a novel. Novels go happiest when you discover something you did not know you knew. Baldwin's experience has shaped his tongue toward directness, for urgency – the honorable defense may be that he has not time nor patience to create characters, milieu, and mood for the revelation of important complexities he has already classified in his mind.

Baldwin's characters maim themselves trying to smash through the wall of their imprisonment. William Burroughs gives what may be the finest record in our century of the complete psychic convict. *Naked Lunch* is a book of pieces and fragments, notes and nightmarish anecdotes, which he wrote – according to his preface – in various states of delirium, going in and out of a heroin addiction. It is not a novel in any conventional sense, but then there's a question whether it's a novel by any set of standards other than the dictum that prose about imaginary people put between book covers is a novel. At any rate, the distinction is not important except for the fact that *Naked Lunch* is next to impossible to read in consecutive fashion. I saw excerpts of it years ago, and thought enough of them to go on record that Burroughs 'may conceivably be possessed by genius.' I still believe that, but it is one thing to be possessed by genius, it is another to be a genius, and *Naked Lunch* read from cover to cover is not as exciting as in its separate pieces. Quantity changes quality, as Karl Marx once put it, and fifty or sixty three-page bits about homosexual orgies, castration, surgeon-assassins, and junkie fuzz dissolving into a creeping green ooze leaves one feeling pretty tough. 'Let's put some blue-purple blood in the next rape,' says your jaded taste.

This is, however, quibbling. Some of the best prose in America is graffiti found on men's-room walls. It is prose written in bone, etched by acid, it is the prose of harsh truth, the virulence of the criminal who never found his stone walls and so settles down on the walls of the john, it is the language of hatred unencumbered by guilt, hesitation, scruple, or complexity. Burroughs must be the greatest writer of graffiti who ever lived. His style has the snap of a whip, and it never relents. Every paragraph is quotable. Here's a jewel among a thousand jewels:

> *Dr Benway . . . looks around and picks up one of those rubber vacuum cups at the end of a stick they use to unstop toilets . . . 'Make an incision, Doctor Limpf . . . I'm going to massage the heart.' . . . Dr Benway washes the suction cup by swishing it around in the toilet-bowl . . .*
>
> *Dr Limpf: 'The incision is ready, doctor.'*
>
> *Dr Benway forces the cup into the incision and works it up and down. Blood spurts all over the doctors, the nurse and the wall . . .*
>
> *Nurse: 'I think she's gone, doctor.'*
>
> *Dr Benway: 'Well, it's all in the day's work.'*

Punch and Judy. Mr Interlocutor and Mr Bones. One, two, three, bam! two, four eight, bam! The drug addict lives with a charge wire so murderous he must hang his nervous system on a void. Burroughs' achievement, his great achievement, is that he has brought back snowflakes from this murderous void.

Once, years ago in Chicago, I was coming down with a bad cold. By accident, a friend took me to hear a jazz musician named Sun Ra who played 'space music'. The music was a little like the sound of Ornette Coleman, but further out, outer space music, close to the FREE of an electric drill at the center of a harsh trumpet. My cold cleared up in five minutes. I swear it. The anger of the sound penetrated into some sprung-up rage which was burning fuel for the cold. Burroughs' pages have the same medicine. If a hundred patients on terminal cancer read *Naked Lunch*, one or two might find remission. Bet money on that. For Burroughs is the surgeon of the novel.

Yet he is something more. It is his last ability which entitles him to a purchase on genius. Through the fantasies runs a vision of a future world, a half-demented welfare state, an abattoir of science fiction with surgeons, bureaucrats, perverts, diplomats, a world not describable short of getting into the book. The ideas have pushed into the frontier of an all-electronic universe. One holds onto a computer in some man-eating machine of the future which has learned to use language. The words come out in squeaks, spiced with static, sex coiled up with technology like a scream on the radar. Bombarded by his language, the sensation is like being in a room where three radios, two television sets, stereo hi-fi, a pornographic movie, and two automatic dishwashers are working at once while a mad scientist conducts the dials to squeeze out the maximum disturbance. If this is a true picture of the world to come, and it may be, then Burroughs is a great writer. Yet there is sadness in reading him, for one gets intimations of a mind which might have come within distance of Joyce, except that a catastrophe has been visited on it, a blow by a sledge hammer, a junkie's needle which left the crystalline brilliance crashed into bits.

Now beyond a doubt, of all the books discussed here, the one which most cheats evaluation is Joseph Heller's *Catch-22*. It was the book which took me longest to finish, and I almost gave it up. Yet I think that a year from now I may remember it more vividly than *The Thin Red Line*. Because it is an original. There's no book like it anyone has read. Yet it's maddening. It reminds one of a Jackson Pollock painting eight feet high, twenty feet long. Like yard goods, one could cut it anywhere. One could take out a hundred pages anywhere from the middle of *Catch-22*, and not even the author could be certain they were gone. Yet the length and similarity of one page to another gives a curious meat-and-potatoes to the madness; building upon itself the book becomes substantial until the last fifty pages grow suddenly and surprisingly powerful, only to be marred by an ending over the last five pages which is hysterical, sentimental and wall-eyed for Hollywood.

This is the skin of the reaction. If I were a major critic, it would be a virtuoso performance to write a definitive piece on *Catch-22*. It would take ten thousand words or more. Because Heller is carrying his reader on a more consistent voyage through Hell than any American writer before him (except Burroughs who has already made the trip and now sells choice seats in the auditorium), and so the analysis of Joseph H.'s Hell would require a discussion of other varieties of inferno and whether they do more than this author's tour.

Catch-22 is a nightmare about an American bomber squadron on a made-up island off Italy. Its hero is a bombardier named Yossarian who has flown fifty missions and wants out. On this premise is tattooed the events of the novel, fifty characters, two thousand frustrations (an average of four or five to the page), and one simple motif: more frustration. Yossarian's colonel wants to impress his general and so raises the number of missions to fifty-five. When the pilots have fifty-four, the figure is lifted to sixty. They are going for eighty by the time the book has been done. On the way every character goes through a routine *on every page* which is as formal as a little peasant figure in a folk dance. Back in school, we had a joke we used to repeat. It went:

'Whom are you talking about?'

'Herbert Hoover.'

'Never heard of him.'

'Never heard of whom?'

'Herbert Hoover.'

'Who's he?'

'He's the man you mentioned.'

'Never heard of Herbert Hoover.'

So it went. So goes *Catch-22*. It's the rock and roll of novels. One finds its ancestor in Basic Training. We were ordered to have clean sheets for Saturday inspection. But one week we were given no clean sheets from the Post laundry so we slept on our mattress covers, which got dirty. After inspection, the platoon was restricted to quarters. 'You didn't have clean sheets,' our sergeant said.

'How could we have clean sheets if the clean sheets didn't come?'

'How do I know?' said the sergeant. 'The regulations say you gotta have clean sheets.'

'But we can't have clean sheets if there are no clean sheets.'

'That,' said the sergeant, 'is tough shit.'

Which is what *Catch-22* should have been called. The Army is a village of colliding bureaucracies whose colliding orders cook up impossibilities. Heller takes this one good joke and exploits it into two thousand variations of the same good joke, but in the act he somehow creates a rational vision of the modern world. Yet the crisis of reason is that it can no longer comprehend the modern world. Heller demonstrates that a rational man devoted to reason must arrive at the conclusion that either the world is mad and he is the only sane man in it, or (and this is the weakness of *Catch-22* – it never explores this possibility) the sane man is not really sane because his rational propositions are without existential reason.

On page 178, there is a discussion about God.

'... *how much reverence can you have for a Supreme Being who finds it necessary to include such phenomena*

> *as phlegm and tooth decay in His divine system of crea-*
> *tion . . . Why in the world did He ever create pain?'*
>   *'Pain?' Lieutenant Scheisskopf's wife pounced upon*
> *the word victoriously. 'Pain is a useful symptom. Pain is a*
> *warning to us of bodily dangers.'*
>   *. . . 'Why couldn't he have used a doorbell instead to*
> *notify us, or one of His celestial choirs?'*

Right there is planted the farthest advance of the flag of reason in his cosmology. Heller does not look for any answer, but there is an answer which might go that God gave us pain for the same reason the discovery of tranquilizers was undertaken by the Devil: if we have an immortal soul some of us come close to it only through pain. A season of sickness can be preferable to a flight from disease, for it discourages the onrush of a death which begins in the center of oneself.

Give talent its due. *Catch-22* is the debut of a writer with merry gifts. Heller may yet become Gogol. But what makes one hesitate to call his first novel great or even major is that he has only grasped the inferior aspect of Hell. What is most unendurable is not the military world of total frustration so much as the midnight frustration of the half world, Baldwin's other country, where a man may have time to hear his soul, and time to go deaf, even be forced to contemplate himself as he becomes deadened before his death. (Much as Hemingway may have been.) That is when one becomes aware of the anguish, the existential *angst*, which wars enable one to forget. It is that other death – without war – where one dies by a failure of nerve, which opens the bloodiest vents of Hell. And that is a novel none of us has yet come back alive to write.

With the exception of *Another Country,* the novels talked about up to now have been books written for men. *Catch-22* was liked, I believe, by almost every man who read it. Women were puzzled. The world of a man is a world of surface slick and rock knowledge. A man must live by daily acts where he goes to work and works on the world some incremental bit, using the tools, instruments, and the techniques of the world. Thus a man cannot afford to go too deeply into the underlying meaning of a single subject. He prefers to become interested in quick proportions and contradictions, in the practical surface of things. A book like *Catch-22* is written on the face of solemn events and their cockeyed contradictions. So it has a vast appeal: it relieves the frustration men feel at the idiocy of their work. *Naked Lunch* fries the surface in a witch's skillet; the joy in reading is equal to the kick of watching a television announcer go insane before your eyes and start to croon obscenely about the President, First Lady, Barry Goldwater, Cardinal Spellman, J. Edgar. Somewhere in America somebody would take out his pistol and shoot the set. Burroughs shatters the surface and blasts its shards into the madness beneath. He rips the reader free of suffocation. Jones wrote a book which a dedicated corporation executive or an ambitious foreman would read with professional avidity because they would learn a bit about the men who work for them. *The Thin Red Line* brings detail to the surprises on the toughest part of the skin. So these three books are, as I say, books for men. Whereas *Another Country*, obsessed with that transcendental divide keeping sex from love, is a book more for women, or for men and women. So too is *Set This House on Fire*. And much the same can be said of *Rabbit, Run* and *Letting Go*.

On record are the opinions of a partisan. So it is necessary to admit that John Updike's novel was approached with animus. His reputation has traveled in convoy up the Avenue of the Establishment, *The New York Times Book Review* blowing sirens like a motorcycle caravan, the professional muse of *The New Yorker* sitting in the Cadillac, membership cards to the right Fellowships in his pocket. The sort of critics who are rarely right about a book –

Arthur Mizener and Granville Hicks, for example – ride on his flanks, literary bodyguards. *Life* Magazine blew its kiss of death into the confetti. To my surprise, *Rabbit, Run* was therefore a better book than I thought it would be. The Literary Establishment was improving its taste. Updike was not simply a junior edition of James Gould Cozzens. But of course the Establishment cannot nominate a candidate coherently. Updike's merits and vices were turned inside out. The good girlish gentlemen of letters were shocked by the explicitness of the sex in *Rabbit, Run,* and slapped him gently for that with their fan, but his style they applauded. It is Updike's misfortune that he is invariably honored for his style (which is atrocious – and smells like stale garlic) and is insufficiently recognized for his gifts. He could become the best of our literary novelists if he could forget about style and go deeper into the literature of sex. *Rabbit, Run* moves in well-modulated spurts at precisely those places where the style subsides to a ladylike murmur and the characters take over. The trouble is that young John, like many a good young writer before him, does not know exactly what to do when action lapses, and so he cultivates his private vice, he *writes.* And there are long overfingered descriptions in exacerbated syntax, airless crypts of four or five pages, huge inner exertion reminiscent of weight lifters, a stale sweet sweat clings to his phrases.

Example: *Redbook, Cosmopolitan, McCall's.*
Boys are playing basketball around a telephone pole with a backboard to it. Legs, shouts. The scrape and snap of Keds on loose alley pebbles seems to catapult their voices high into the moist March air blue above the wires. Rabbit Angstrom, coming up the alley in a business suit, stops and watches, though he's twenty-six and six-three. So tall, he seems an unlikely rabbit, but the breadth of white face, the pallor of his blue irises, and a nervous flutter under his brief nose as he stabs a cigarette into his mouth partially explain the nickname.

Example: *True Confessions.*

Outside in the air his fears condense. Globes of ether, pure nervousness, slide down his legs. The sense of outside space scoops at his chest.

Example: *Elements of Grammar.*

His hands lift of their own and he feels the wind on his ears even before, his heels hitting heavily on the pavement at first but with an effortless gathering out of a kind of sweet panic growing lighter and quicker and quieter, he runs. Ah: runs. Runs.

It's the rare writer who cannot have sentences lifted from his work, but the first quotation is taken from the first five sentences of the book, the second is on the next-to-last page, and the third is nothing less than the last three sentences of the novel. The beginning and end of a novel are usually worked over. They are the index to taste in the writer. Besides, trust your local gangster. In the run of Updike's pages are one thousand other imprecise, flatulent, wry-necked, precious, overpreened, self-indulgent, tortured sentences. It is the sort of prose which would be admired in a writing course overseen by a fussy old nance. And in Updike's new book, *The Centaur*, which was only sampled, the style has gotten worse. Pietisms are congregating, affirmations à la Archibald MacLeish.

The pity is that Updike has instincts for finding the heart of the conventional novel, that still-open no man's land between the surface and the deep, the soft machinery of the world and the subterranean rigors of the dream. His hero, Rabbit Angstrom, is sawed in two by the clear anguish of watching his private vision go at a gallop away from the dread real weight of his responsibility. A routine story of a man divided between a dull wife he cannot bear to live with and a blowsy tough tender whore he cannot make it with, the merit of the book is not in the simplicity of its problem, but in the dread Updike manages to convey, despite the literary commercials in the style, of a young man who is beginning to lose nothing less than his good American soul, and yet it is not quite his fault. The power of the novel comes from a sense, not absolutely unworthy of Thomas Hardy, that the universe hangs over our fates like a great sullen hopeless sky. There is real pain in the book, and a touch of awe. It is a novel which could have been important, it could have had a chance to stay alive despite its mud pies in prose, but at the very end the book drowns in slime. Updike does not know how to finish. Faced with the critical choice of picking one woman or another (and by the end, both women are in fearful need), his character bolts over a literal hill and runs away. Maybe he'll be back tomorrow, maybe he'll never be back, but a decision was necessary. The book ends as minor, a pop-out. One is left with the expectation that Updike will never be great; there is something too fatally calculated about his inspiration. But very good he can be, a good writer of the first rank with occasional echoes from the profound. First he must make an enemy or two of the commissioners on the Literary Mafia. Of course a man spends his life trying to get up his guts for such a caper.

Letting Go, by Philip Roth, has precisely the opposite merits and faults. As a novel, its strategy is silly, tiresome, and weak. But its style, while not noteworthy, is decent and sometimes, in dialogue, halfway nice. It is good time spent to read any ten pages in the book. The details are observed, the mood is calm, the point is always made. It is like having an affair with a pleasant attentive woman – the hours go by neatly. It is only at the end of a year that one may realize the preoccupations of the mistress are hollow, and the seasons have been wasted.

Letting Go is a scrupulous account in upper Jewish New Yorker genre of a few years in the lives of two English department college instructors, one married to the most coveted of creatures, a fragile dreary hang-up of a heroine, the other a bachelor and lover of worried proportions. Very little happens. The wife goes on being herself, the husband remains naturally frozen and stingy, and the instructor-lover has a small literary breakdown. One can say, well isn't this life? Didn't Chekhov and de Maupassant write about such things? And the answer is yes they did, in five pages they did, and caught that mood which reminds us that there is sadness in attrition and grinding sorrows for decency. But Roth is not writing a book with a vision of life; on the contrary, one could bet a grand he is working out an obsession. His concentration is appropriated by something in his life which has been using him up in the past. Virtually every writer, come soon or late, has a cramped-up love affair which is all but hopeless. *Of Human Bondage* could be the case study of half the writers who ever lived. But the obsession is opposed to art in the same way a compulsive talker is opposed to good conversation. The choice is either to break the obsession or enter it. The compulsive talker must go through the herculean transformation of learning to quit or must become a great monologuist. Roth tried to get into the obsession – he gave six hundred pages to wandering around in a ten-page story – but he did it without courage. He was too careful not to get hurt on his trip and so he does not reveal himself: he does not *dig*. The novel skitters like a water fly from pollen spread to pollen spread; a series of good short stories accumulate en route, but no novel. The iron law of the conventional novel, the garden novel, is that the meaning of the action must grow on every page or else the book will wither. It is Updike's respectable achievement in *Rabbit, Run* that he writes just such a book, or tries to until the last three pages when he vanishes like a sneak thief. Roth never gets into the game. One senses a determined fight to maintain *Letting Go* as a collection of intricately intercollected short stories.

But the short story has a tendency to look for climates of permanence – an event occurs, a man is hurt by it in some small way forever. The novel moves as naturally toward flux. An event occurs, a man is injured, and a month later is working on something else. The short story likes to be classic. It is most acceptable when one fatal point is made. Whereas the novel is dialectical. It is most alive when one can trace the disasters which follow victory or the subtle turns that sometimes come from a defeat. A novel can be created out of short stories only if the point in each story is consecutively more interesting and incisive than the point before it, when the author in effect is drilling for oil. But Roth's short stories in *Letting Go* just dig little holes in many suburban lawns until finally the work of reading it becomes almost as depressing as must have been the work of writing it. Roth has to make a forced march in his next book, or at least, like Updike, get around to putting his foot in the whorehouse door. If he doesn't, a special Hell awaits his ambition – he will be called the Rich Man's Paddy Chayefsky, and Paddy without his grasp of poverty is nothing much at all.

It is necessary to say that the four stories about the Glass family by J. D. Salinger, published in two books called *Franny and Zooey* and *Raise High the Roof Beam, Carpenters*, seem to have been written for high-school girls. The second piece in the second book, called *Seymour – An Introduction*, must be the most slovenly portion of prose ever put out by an important American writer. It is not even professional Salinger. Salinger at his customary worst, as here in the other three stories of the two books, is never bad – he is just disappointing. He stays too long on the light ice of his gift, writes exquisite dialogue and creates minor moods with sweetness and humor, and never gives the fish its hook. He disappoints because he is always practicing. But when he dips into Seymour, the Glass brother who committed suicide, when the cult comes to silence before the appearance of the star – the principal, to everyone's horror, has nausea on the stage. Salinger for the first time is engaged in run-off writing, free suffragette prose; his inhibitions (which once helped by their restraint to create his style) are now stripped. He is giving you himself as he is. No concealment. It feels like taking a bath in a grease trap.

Now, all of us have written as badly. There are nights when one comes home after a cancerously dull party, full of liquor but not drunk, leaden with boredom, somewhere out in Fitzgerald's long dark night. Writing at such a time is like making love at such a time. It is hopeless, it desecrates one's future, but one does it anyway because at least it is an act. Such writing is almost always unsprung. It is reminiscent of the wallflower who says, 'To hell with inhibitions, I'm going to dance.' The premise is that what comes out is valid because it is the record of a mood. So one records the mood. What a mood. Full of vomit, self-pity, panic, paranoia, megalomania, *merde*, whimpers, excuses, turns of the neck, flips of the wrist, transports. It is the bends of Hell. If you purge it, if you get sleep and tear it up in the morning, it can do no more harm than any other bad debauch. But Salinger went ahead and reread his stew, then sent it to *The New Yorker*, and they accepted it. Now, several years later, he reprints it in book covers.

There is social process at work here. Salinger was the most gifted minor writer in America. *The New Yorker's* ability is to produce such writers. The paradox comes from the social fact that *The New Yorker* is a major influence on American life. Hundreds of thousands, perhaps millions of people in the most established parts of the middle class kill their quickest impulses before they dare to act in such a way as to look ridiculous to the private eye of their taste whose style has been keyed by the eye of *The New Yorker*. Salinger was the finest writer *The New Yorker* ever produced, but profoundly minor. The major writer like James Jones, indeed James Jones, leads the kind of inner life which enables him to study victories as well as defeats; Salinger was catapulted by a study of excruciating small defeats into a position of major importance. The phenomenon in the nation was the same those years. Men of minor abilities engaged America in major brinkmanships.

But it is always dangerous when the Literary Mafia (*The New Yorker*, the *Saturday Review*, *The New York Times Book Review*, *Time* Magazine's book reviews, and the genteel elements in publishing) promote a minor writer into a major writer. A vested interest attaches itself to keeping the corpse of the violated standards buried. Readers who might be average keen in their sense of literary value find their taste mucked up. The greatest damage in this case, however, seems to have been to Salinger himself. Because a writer, with aristocratic delicacy of intent and nerves so subtle that only isolation makes life bearable for him, has been allowed to let his talent fester in that corrupt isolation. Salinger has been the most important writer in America for a generation of adolescents and college students. He was their leader in exile. The least he owed them for his silence was a major performance.

But it's a rare man who can live like a hermit and produce a major performance unless he has critics who are near to him and hard on him. No friend who worried about Salinger's future should have let him publish *Seymour – An Introduction* in *The New Yorker* without daring to lose his friendship first by telling him how awful it was. Yet there was too much depending on Salinger's interregnum – he was so *inoffensive*, finally. So a suspension of the critical faculty must have gone on in the institutional wheels of *The New Yorker* which was close to psychotic in its evasions.

As for the other three stories in the two books, they are not as good as the stories in *Nine Stories*. Affectations which were part once of Salinger's charm are now faults. An excessive desire to please runs through his pages. There is too much sweetness. He is too pleased with himself, too nice, he lingers too much over the happy facility of his details in a way Fitzgerald never would. He is no longer a writer so much as he is an entertainer, a slim much-beloved version of Al Jolson or Sophie Tucker; the music hall is in the root of his impulse as much as the dungeons and mansions of literature. Does one desire the real irony? There is nothing in

Franny and Zooey which would hinder it from becoming first-rate television. It is genre with all the limitations of genre: catalogs of items in the medicine chest, long intimate family conversations with life, snap with mother, crackle and pop. If I were a television producer I'd put on *Franny and Zooey* tomorrow. And indeed in ten years they will. America will have moved from *One Man's Family* to the *Glass Family*. Which is progress. I'd rather have the Glass family on the air. But don't confuse the issue. The Glass stories are not literature, but television. And Salinger's work since *The Catcher in the Rye* is part of his long retreat from what is substantial, agonizing, uproarious, or close to awe and terror. *The Catcher in the Rye* was able to change people's lives. The new books are not even likely to improve the conversation in college dormitories. It is time Salinger came back to the city and got his hands dirty with a rough corruption or two, because the very items which composed the honor of his reputation, his resolute avoidance of the mass media and society, have now begun to back up on him. There is a taste of something self-absorptive, narcissistic, even putrefactive in his long contemplation of a lintless navel.

The value of past predictions by this critic may be judged by the following about Saul Bellow. It is taken from page 467 in *Advertisements for Myself.*

> *When and if I come to read* Henderson the Rain King, *let me hope I do not feel the critic's vested interest to keep a banished writer in limbo, for I sense uneasily that without reading it, I have already the beginnings of a negative evaluation for it since I doubt that I would believe in Henderson as a hero.*

Well, one might as well eat the crow right here. Henderson is an exceptional character, almost worthy of Gulliver or Huckleberry Finn, and it is possible that of all the books mentioned in this piece, *Henderson the Rain King* comes the closest to being a great novel. Taken even by its smallest dimension, and its final failure, it will still become a classic, a fine curiosity of a book quite out of the main stream of American letters but a classic in the way *The Innocents Abroad*, or *The Ox-Bow Incident*, *The Informer* or *A High Wind in Jamaica* is classic.

Bellow's main character, Henderson, is a legendary giant American, an eccentric millionaire, six-four in height, with a huge battered face, an enormous chest, a prodigious pot-belly, a wild crank's gusto for life, and a childlike impulse to say what he thinks. He is a magical hybrid of Jim Thorpe and Dwight Macdonald. And he is tormented by an inner voice which gives him no rest and poisons his marriages and pushes him to go forth. So he chooses to go to Africa (after first contemplating a visit to the Eskimos) and finds a native guide to take him deep into the interior.

The style gallops like Henderson, full of excess, full of light, loaded with irritating effusions, but it is a style which moves along. *The Adventures of Augie March* was written in a way which could only be called *all writing*. That was one of the troubles with the book. Everything was mothered by the style. But Henderson talks in a free-swinging easy bang-away monologue which puts your eye in the center of the action. I don't know if Bellow ever visited Africa, I would guess he didn't, but his imaginative faculty – which has always been his loot – pulls off a few prodigies. I don't know if any other American writer has done Africa so well. As for instance:

> *I was in tremendous shape those first long days, hot as they were. At night, after Romilayu had prayed, and we lay on the ground, the face of the air breathed back on us, breath for breath. And then there were the calm stars, turning around and singing, and the birds of the night with heavy bodies, fanning by. I couldn't have asked for anything better. When I laid my ear to the ground, I*

thought I could hear hoofs. It was like lying on the skin of a drum.

After a series of tragicomic adventures, Henderson reaches a royal almost Oriental tribe with a culture built upon magic and death. He is brought to the King, Dahfu, who lives in a wooden palace attended by a harem of beautiful Amazons. (One could be visiting the royalest pad in Harlem. Dahfu is a philosopher-king, large in size, noble, possessed of grace, complex, dignified, elegant, educated, living suspended between life and death. The King, delighted with his new friend, takes him into the secrets of his mind and his palace, and one begins to read the book with a vast absorption because Bellow is now inching more close to the Beast of mystery than any American novelist before him. Dahfu is an exceptional creation, a profoundly sophisticated man with a deep acceptance of magic, an intellectual who believes that civilization can be saved only by a voyage back into the primitive, an expedition which he is of course uniquely suited to lead.

As the action explores its way down into an underworld of plot and magical omens, one ceases to know any longer whether Dahfu is potentially an emperor who can save the world, or a noble man lost in a Faustian endeavor. The book is on the threshold of a stupendous climax – for the first time in years I had the feeling I was going to learn something large from a novel – and then like a slow leak the air goes out of the book in the last fifty pages. Dahfu is killed in a meaningless action, Henderson goes home to his wife, and the mystery that Bellow has begun to penetrate closes over his book, still intact.

He is a curious writer. He has the warmest imagination, I think, of any writer in my generation, and this gift leads him to marvelous places – it is possible that Bellow succeeds in telling us more about the depths of the black man's psyche than either Baldwin or Ellison. He has a widely cultivated mind which nourishes his gift. He has a facility for happy surprises, and in Henderson, unlike Augie March, he has developed a nose for where the treasure is buried. Yet I still wonder if he is not too timid to become a great writer. A novelist like Jones could never have conceived *Henderson the Rain King* (no more could I), but I know that Jones or myself would have been ready to urinate blood before we would have been ready to cash our profit and give up as Bellow did on the possibilities of a demonically vast ending. The clue to this capitulation may be detected in Bellow's one major weakness, which is that he creates individuals and not relations between them, at least not yet. Augie March travels alone, the hero of *Seize the Day* is alone, Henderson forms passionate friendships but they tend to get fixed and the most annoying aspect of the novel is the constant repetition of the same sentiments, as if Bellow is knocking on a door of meaning which will not open for him. It is possible that the faculty of imagination is opposed to the gift of grasping relationships – in the act of coming to know somebody else well, the point of the imagination may be dulled by the roughness of the other's concrete desires and the attrition of living not only in one's own boredom but someone else's. Bellow has a lonely gift, but it is a gift. I would guess he is more likely to write classics than major novels, which is a way of saying that he will give intense pleasure to particular readers over the years, but is not too likely to seize the temper of our time and turn it.

For those who like the results of a horse race, it should be clear that the novels I liked the most in this round of reading were *Henderson, Naked Lunch,* and *Catch-22. The Thin Red Line* if not inspired was still impressive. *Another Country* suffered from too little style but compensated by its force. *Rabbit, Run* was better than expected but cloyed by too much writing. *Set This House on Fire* was rich in separate parts, and obese for the whole. *Letting Go* gave a demonstration of brilliant tactics and no novelistic strategy at all. *Franny and Zooey* and *Raise High the Roof Beam, Carpenters* was a literary scandal which came in last.

It has been said more than once that Tolstoy and Dostoevsky divided the central terrain of the modern novel between them. Tolstoy's concern – even in the final pessimism of *The Kreutzer Sonata* – was with men-in-the-world, and indeed the panorama of his books carries to us an image of a huge landscape peopled with figures who changed that landscape, whereas the bulk of Dostoevsky's work could take place in ten closed rooms: it is not society but a series of individuals we remember, each illuminated by the terror of exploring the mystery of themselves. This distinction is not a final scheme for classifying the novel. If one can point to *Moby Dick* as a perfect example of a novel in the second category – a book whose action depends upon the voyage of Ahab into his obsession – and to *An American Tragedy* as a virile example of the first kind of novel, one must still come up short before the work of someone like Henry James, who straddles the categories, for he explores into society as if the world were a creature in a closed room and he could discover its heart. Yet the distinction is probably the most useful single guide we have to the novel and can even be given a modern application to Proust as a novelist of the developed, introspective, but still objective world, and Joyce as a royal, demented, most honorable traveler through the psyche. The serious novel begins from a fixed philosophical point – the desire to discover reality – and it goes to search for that reality in society, or else must embark on a trip up the upper Amazon of the inner eye.

It is this necessity to travel into one direction or the other up to the end which makes the writing of novels fatal for one's talent and finally for one's health, as the horns of a bull are final doom for the suit of lights. If one explores the world, one's talent must be blunted by punishment, one's artistic integrity by corruption: nobody can live in the world without shaking the hand of people he despises; so, an ultimate purity must be surrendered. Yet it is as dangerous to travel unguided into the mysteries of the Self, for insanity prepares an ambush. No man explores into his own nature without submitting to a curse from the root of biology since existence would cease if it were natural to turn upon oneself.

This difficulty has always existed for the novelist, but today it may demand more antithesis and more agony than before. The writer who would explore the world must encounter a society which is now conscious of itself, and so resistant (most secretly) to an objective eye. Detours exist everywhere. There was a time when a writer had to see just a little bit of a few different faces in the world and could know that the world was still essentially so simple and so phrased that he might use his imagination to fill in unknown colors in the landscape. Balzac could do that, and so could Zola. But the arts of the world suffered a curious inversion as man was turned by the twentieth century into mass man rather than democratic man. The heartland which was potential in everyone turned upon itself; people used their personal arts to conceal from themselves the nature of their work. They chose to become experts rather than artists. The working world was no longer a panorama of factories and banks so much as it was reminiscent of hospitals and plastic recreation centers. Society tended to collect in small stagnant pools. Now, any young man trying to explore that world is held up by pleasures which are not sufficiently intense to teach him and is dulled by injustices too elusive to fire his rage. The Tolstoyan novel begins to be impossible. Who can create a vast canvas when the imagination must submit itself to a plethora of detail in each joint of society? Who can travel to many places when the complexity of each pool sucks up one's attention like a carnivorous cess-fed flower? Of all the writers mentioned here, only Jones, Heller and Burroughs even try to give a picture of the world, and the last two have departed from conventional reality before financing the attempt. It may be that James Jones is indeed the single major American writer capable of returning with a realistic vision of the complex American reality. But by his method, because of the progressively increasing confusion and contradiction of each separate corner in American society, he will have to write twenty or thirty books before he will have sketched even a small design.

Yet a turn in the other direction, into the world of the Self, is not less difficult. An intellectual structure which is cancerous and debilitating to the instinct of the novelist inhabits the crossroads of the inner mind. Psychoanalysis. An artist must not explore into himself with language given by another. A vocabulary of experts is a vocabulary greased out and sweated in committee and so is inimical to a private eye. One loses what is new by confusing it with what may be common to others. The essential ideas of psychoanalysis are reductive and put a dead weight on the confidence of the venture. If guilt, for example, is neurotic, a clumsy part of the functioning in a graceful machine, then one does not feel like a hero studying his manacles, nor a tragic victim regarding his just sentence, but instead is a skilled mechanic trying to fix his tool. Brutally, simply, mass man cannot initiate an inner voyage unless it is conducted by an expert graduated by an institution.

Set This House on Fire, Another Country, Rabbit, Run, Letting Go, Henderson, and the Glass stories were all amateur expeditions into the privacy of the Self, but they are also a measure of the difficulty, because one could sense the exhaustion of talent in the fires on the way, as if a company of young untried men were charging a hill which was mined and laid across with fire lanes for automatic weapons.

Yet the difficulty goes beyond the country of psychoanalysis. There are hills beyond that hill. The highest faces an abyss. Man in the Middle Ages or the Renaissance, man even in the nineteenth century, explored deep into himself that he might come closer to a vision of a God or some dictate from eternity, but that exploration is suspect in itself today, and in the crucial climactic transcendental moments of one's life, there is revealed still another dilemma. God, is it God one finds, or madness?

The religious temper of these books is significant. Of them all, only *The Thin Red Line, Naked Lunch, Another Country,* and *Letting Go* have no overt religious pre-occupation. Yet altogether one could make a kind of case that *Naked Lunch* and *Another Country* are not divorced from religious obsessions. The suggestion of still another frontier for the American novel is here. A war has been fought by some of us over the last fifteen years to open the sexual badlands to our writing, and that war is in the act of being won. Can one now begin to think of an attack on the stockade – those dead forts where the spirit of twentieth-century man, frozen in flop and panic before the montage of his annihilation, has collected, like castrated cattle behind the fence? Can the feet of those infantrymen of the arts, the novelists, take us through the mansions and the churches into the palace of the Bitch where the real secrets are stored? We are the last of the entrepreneurs, and one of us homeless guns had better make it, or the future will smell like the dead air of the men who captured our time during that huge collective cowardice which was the aftermath of the Second War.

PART THREE: RESPITES

Our Argument Somewhat Continued

*Two interviews follow. They are in fact three, for the first
piece consists of two interviews done a season apart, but put
together here. This first piece, here titled 'Petty Notes on
Some Sex in America', was done for* Playboy, *for two* Play-
boy *panels with the formidable titles 'Sex and Censorship in
Literature and the Arts', starring Maurice Girodias, Barney
Rosset, Otto Preminger, Norman Mailer, Ralph Ginz-
burg, Thurman Arnold, and Albert Ellis, and 'The
Womanization of America', billing Dr Theodor Reik, Alex-
ander King, Dr Ashley Montague, Mort Sahl, Edward
Bernays, Dr Ernest Dichter, Herbert Mayes, myself again.
The panels, like* Playboy, *are overprocessed. The editors
formulated questions (in a style you will be presented soon
enough), gave them to the* Realist's *Reichsmarschall Paul
Krassner, who was obliged to interview me by reading Herr*
Playboy's *questions, and your author's answers were then
collated by the editors into the panel – the panelists all sep-
arately interviewed, but with all answers interlocked to give
the impression the eight gents were in one room at the same
time all working for* Playboy. *The result is flatulent. For
most of the Symposium, nobody answers anybody else; no
real reactions – just replies at a tangent to pretend to satisfy
the needs of a supposed collective dialogue which was never
collective, and one's answers were chopped up, the questions
were shifted, parts of the answers were dropped forever. My
necessity, here, then, was to reconstitute – if able – my indi-
vidual interviews, and I've touched them up in order to try
to find the original flavor, the original cheerless flavor of
answering Herr Krassner von der Realismus while he asked
me questions worked up by a Spectorsky committee. A pity,
for the answers are sufficiently sensible to reproduce here,*

although singularly charmless. Wit is altogether absent. Sol-
emnity pervades.

The other interview was done for Paris Review's *Writers
at Work series and the questions were gathered by the
honorable Steven Marcus who worked up a careful structure
for his questions so that the interview built in the interest of
a reader as it progressed, and some rudiments of style were
present in my answer. It has been cut by two-thirds for its
show here since the early portions were autobiographical
and have no bearing on the affairs of this book; what
remains is about the art of writing in general, thus it touches
on the plague.*

*But note my emphasis. The first interview, the double
panel interview, is sound, but dispiriting in tone, not I grant
you so dispiriting as reading an article in* Harper's *while
sipping Alka-Seltzer, but still dialogue in which no living
human can feel pride. The other, the* Paris Review *interview,
although later fortified by specific questions from the
editors (which broke the spell) and worked on stylistically by
me at home (which broke the integrity), has nonetheless a
unity of voice which came out of the critical and careful
nature of a clear confrontation.*

*There is everywhere now a passion to dislocate the mood
of an event, to remove it from the site of its confrontation.
Any reader of the original* Playboy *panel must have felt
uneasy at the center of his perceptions all the while he was
reading, since the panel never had a physical existence. That
leaves a trace of the void. Especially if one is not told.
Similarly, a show on television at midnight, taped two hours
before, induces a slipping at the base of one's perception of
time. Style is root. The tension in the years of the plague is
to cut the root and wait for style to expire or accelerate itself
into the grandiloquent. If Camp is the flower on this plague,
the first interview to follow falls into a form which has yet
no name, some sturdy vegetable and weed of the plague,
common as the intelligence of a newspaper column, liberal*

in tone but totalitarian as a lack of bell-bottom trousers at her highness' ball.

Petty Notes on Some Sex in America

PLAYBOY

In G. Legman's classic study of censorship, *Love and Death*, he says: 'Murder is a crime. Describing murder is not. Sex is not a crime. Describing sex is. Why?'

MAILER

I don't know that I have the answer offhand, but I think one possibility is this: reading about murder very often *voids* the desire, whereas reading about sex often *increases* the desire. Now it's obvious that censors are not interested in increasing the amount of sexual desire in a country. There seems to be some relation between high sexuality and low productive level. Countries with the most sexuality have the lowest productive level. In countries like India, where poor people – not intellectuals – are absorbed in sex, productivity has stayed at a very low level for centuries. The same was true in China, and in a lesser sense, perhaps, in Russia before the revolution. At any rate, there does seem to be some relation between sexual repression and the increase of productivity. Censors often feel that they are guarding the *health* of the nation by repressing sexuality.

PLAYBOY

It used to be said, in the book-publishing business – and only partly in jest – that the banning of a book in Boston was a better sales stimulant than a dozen full-page ads. Yet there does exist a kind of tacit censorship, by an author who wants to stay out of trouble, and by his publisher, who may have the same motives, or who may hope for a book that it will be 'pure' enough to be acceptable to a major book club, thus earning more money for himself and his author. Do you find this kind of voluntary or tacit censorship among book publishers?

MAILER

It's not so much a matter of censorship as embarrassment. Often publishers consider certain sexual writing in bad taste. They may often try, with the best intentions, to censor a book because they feel they have the author's interest in mind. They may know very well that certain important reviewers are going to be repelled by certain chapters or passages, and it's going to hurt the reviews they give the book.

As a practical matter, it's even true that there are many reviewers, especially for the smaller newspapers, who don't dare give a book a good review if the sexual material is too intense, too direct, too explicit, because, if they do, they're going to get into trouble with their newspapers. There will be readers writing in to the editor. Of course, it may not even be as direct as that. There may be just a general air of displeasure that the reviewer chose to approve of the book. The result is the sort of censorship that I call *motherly* censorship. The people who do the censoring consider it distasteful, but they're doing it for the child's – in this case, the author's – own good. For that reason, it's the most insidious kind of censorship, for people who are censoring you very often are your friends; they like you, they feel they're doing it for your good, and so it's harder to fight back. You're not able to say to yourself, 'This censor is my enemy and I resist him and take my stand here.' Instead, you have to argue with a close friend whom you've worked with for years, who may even have a certain practical wisdom in what he's saying. So it weakens the writer, vis-à-vis the publisher, and many of the more compromised, more reflective, more sensitive, more timorous parts of his nature are brought forth, and it's harder for him to fight back. Of course, my feeling is that a short gain is taken for a long loss. It's no good for a writer to retract anything he's written that's good.

I would argue with the censor on his own ground that there's no use trying to resist a wave of real interest and even perhaps of biological intensity by trying to suppress it. If there's going to be any censorship – and I'm not certain there should be – it ought to recognize that an intimate and serious evocation of sex is part of the very *marrow* of a nation's culture, and when the marrow is drained through brutal or stupid censorship, then the country begins to sicken. I won't say it *causes*, but it certainly *accelerates*, the sickness of the country.

PLAYBOY

J. Edgar Hoover has stated: 'We know that in an overwhelmingly large number of cases, sex crime is associated with pornography. We know that sex criminals read it, are clearly influenced by it. I believe pornography is a major cause of sex violence. I believe that if we can eliminate the distribution of such items among impressionable children, we shall greatly reduce our frightening crime rate.'

MAILER

There's a subterranean impetus toward pornography so powerful that half the business world is juiced by the sort of half sex that one finds in advertisements. You get enormously attractive girls selling cigarettes, which is a perversion of sex because an enormously attractive girl should be presented for what she is, and not as a handmaiden to a little box containing some paper, tobacco and cellophane.

I think this bad 'art' that one gets in the mass media, on television, in the movies, does the nation far more harm than if one were to remove all controls from pornography and obscenity. Being half excited and half frustrated leads to violence. Whenever one is aroused sexually and doesn't find a consummation, the sex in one's veins turns literally to violence. It's no accident that most frigid people are sadistic.

I refuse to take pornography seriously as a danger to the country until the things that are really dangerous to the country – like the mass media – are subjected to a little scrutiny. When *they're* ready to clean *their* house, I'll say we writers will be ready to clean our house. Of course there are books that don't have a drop of pornography in them that are also evil. I think a reasonably good play on television that is truthful for the first two acts and becomes completely false in the third act is evil, because it arouses certain expectations in people, makes them start considering their lives, and just at the point when they're most open they're turned away with a lie. It's exactly like *coitus interruptus. Coitus interruptus* is evil.

PLAYBOY

One of the evils of pornography, according to James Jackson Kilpatrick in his book *The Smut Peddlers*, is that 'when a youth accepts the idea of sex without love he is stained inside.'

MAILER

The stimulus to pornography is that few people in the country really find love. Because they don't find it, the only way they can begin to get back on the track of finding it is to find some excitation. I think what happens over the years is that most people in America sink sooner or later into a profound depression about sex. They've failed at it so many times in so many ways. Pornography at least charges their batteries, and they go out again, and they search for it again, and again they fail. The argument, I think, comes down to this: that the half state of acceptance America has for pornography is probably intolerable. The tragedy of many people is that they don't find love not because their bodies are inadequate to love, but their minds are. Love is an enormously complex matter, and we have absolutely no preparation for it in this country.

NOTE:
By now, I think the point has been made. It is needless to go on with the interview as a pure interview. I will cut what

remains and give a few worked-over parts. More often than not, the questions from Playboy *will also be deleted.*

ON LADY CHATTERLEY

I read *Lady Chatterley's Lover* in college. The unabridged edition. In the Treasure Room at Widener. It changed my life. It was the first thing I'd ever read that gave me the idea sex could have beauty. I learned from Lawrence that the way to write about sex was not to strike poses, but be true to the logic of each moment. There's a subtle logic of love. I think one of the reasons people are absorbed in love is because it's one of the only ways in which they can find a logic to their lives. Looking back on it now, I think *Lady Chatterley's Lover* is not a very good book. It's probably one of the greatest of the bad books – it's much too simple – it tries to capture the essence of sex and yet has nothing to say about the violence which is part of sex. One doesn't arrive at love by getting into bed with a woman and getting better and better at it, and exploring more and more deeply. A man and woman can't *just* explore more and more deeply into one another. Any number of things keep happening – the world keeps impinging on sex. The lovers keep testing one another; lovers not only create but they also destroy one another; lovers change one another; lovers resist the change that each gives to the other. Lawrence, by voiding these problems, wrote a book that was more mythical than novelistic and terribly sentimental. Yet, it's a book I would defend to the death. If it had entered the general literature at the time it was written, our sexual literature today would be better, more subtle, sensitive, profound. It was exactly because *Lady Chatterley's Lover* was kept in a state of suppression for many years that it took on a power it didn't really possess.

ON TROPIC OF CANCER

What is marvelous about *Tropic of Cancer* is that it is the exact opposite of Lawrence. *Tropic of Cancer* gets the beauty of sex another way, the way people who care a great deal about prize fighting can go to a club fight and enjoy all of it, the ugliness; the blood, the cigar smoke, the spit on the floor, the body odor; it's all part of something whose end is unforeseen. In *Lady Chatterley's Lover*, as I remember, there was not even a description of Mellors' cottage – you don't know what the bed's like – but when you read about sex in Miller, you know how the sheets scratch. For anyone who's interested in getting sexual pleasure from a book, *Tropic of Cancer* is more exciting than *Lady Chatterley's Lover*. When one reads Lawrence there's a certain wistfulness, one feels. Most people don't find sex that pure, that deep, that organic. They find it sort of partial and hot and ugly and fascinating and filled with all sorts of day-to-day details. I'd like to achieve something *between* Miller and Lawrence.

ON THE WOMANIZATION OF AMERICA

Before World War II, America was not a place engaged in world history, but an island *sheltered* from world history, a place where people could go and be free of the deteriorating effects of the crises of history. But when America became a world power and began to have ambitions to become the only world power, American men began to want something else: not to be successful in the old way of building large families, a business, moving into new country, into the frontier, creating something that was going to expand; but rather, living in a relatively stratified society now, they wanted to rise through these strata and acquire more and more power in a world no longer open and viable but on the contrary like an enormously subtle and complex machine. Well, when they desired this, they began to look for something different in women. I think the womanization of America comes not only because women are becoming more selfish, more greedy, less romantic, less warm, more lusty, and more filled with hate – but because the men have collaborated with them. There's been a change in the minds of most men about the function of marriage – it isn't that

they're necessarily becoming weaker vis-à-vis their wives, it's that they've married women who will be less good for them in the home and more good for them in the world. The kind of woman who doesn't wash a dish is usually a beauty who'll spend 10 to 12 hours in bed and will take two hours to make up; she has to have a nurse for the children, but she'll be a wow at a party and will aid the man in his career because when they both go to the party, everybody envies him, covets his woman, so forth. What he wants is a marvelous courtesan with social arts. A courtesan who can go out into the world with him.

ON CHIVALRY

Chivalry consists of opening a door for a woman; that means you've got to be alert, you can't retire for a moment into your own preoccupations. There you are: in position to open the door. The irony is that women who get the kind of man who's marvelous at these small attentions are always profoundly dissatisfied by his lack of depth. When they get a man with depth, they are miserable at his incapacity to take care of them in small ways.

MEN DOING THE HOUSEKEEPING

The fact that men are washing dishes doesn't necessarily mean we are in the final womanization of America; there been, as I said, a shift in the social and biological function of the woman. She is now expected not to create a home much as to be aide-de-camp or staff general to an ambitious opportunist. Part of the unspoken contract is that therefore she won't wash a dish. She won't wash it because she realizes that's not a necessary part of her present function. Her husband would love her to wash the dishes, but he knows damn well she won't, because the kind of women who can serve courtesans and/or aide-de-camps don't wash dishes.

PLAYBOY

What do you think of this remark by Dr Ernest D

founder and president of the Institute for Motivational Research? 'We recently did a study in one of the European countries on birth control . . . There's a definite relationship between the social class and the use of birth-control techniques. I am talking primarily about the lower-income group . . . Our statistical knowledge with the birth-control association has shown that the instruction reaches primarily the middle class and upper-middle class. The real problem is reaching the lower-income-group people, for they are the ones who have many children.'

MAILER

Well, that's the trouble with motivational research. There's no attempt to consider the possibility that a woman might be right – biologically right, instinctively right – in *not* wanting to use a contraceptive. If you take ignorant women, they're not going to be able to express themselves at all. Their reasons for not wanting to use birth-control pills would be rather vague. Suppose unconsciously they feel a deep biological aversion to having sex without the possibility of conceiving. Maybe a woman obtains her deepest knowledge of herself and of the world by the way in which she conceives. You see, the fact that she *can* conceive alters the existential character of her sex. It makes it deeper. She's taking more of a risk. It's more dangerous, more responsible, it's graver. Because it's graver, it's deeper. Since it's deeper, it's better. The reason she may not want to use a contraceptive is because she senses somewhere within her – in dim fashion, no doubt – that there's something alien to the continuation of her, her species, and her family, if she uses a contraceptive. Yet she may also feel a great shame about all this, because, after all, here's this very impressive gentleman with the eyeglasses, taking down every word she says, and there's the attitude of her husband and all the people around her, and her children, about using contraceptives, and so she begins to feel that, well, maybe she's wrong, and confusion is the result. And this pitiful confu-

sion is immediately processed into statistics, which are psychotic in their lack of attachment to the biological reality.

ON HOMOSEXUALITY

I think there may be more homosexuals today than there were fifty years ago. If so, the basic reason might have to do with a general loss of faith in the country, faith in the meaning of one's work, faith in the notion of oneself as a man. When a man can't find any dignity in his work, he loses virility. Masculinity is not something given to you, something you're born with, but something you gain. And you gain it by winning small battles with honor. Because there is very little honor left in American life, there is a certain built-in tendency to destroy masculinity in American men. The mass media, for instance – television first, movies second, magazines third, and newspapers running no poor fourth – tend to destroy virility slowly and steadily. They give people an unreal view of life. They give people a notion that American life is easier than it really is, less complex, more rewarding. The result is that Americans, as they emerge from adolescence into young manhood, are very much like green soldiers being sent into difficult terrain ignorant of the conditions. A lot of virility immediately gets massacred.

PLAYBOY

Does the future of American womanhood – and manhood – really bode ill, or can we hope for a gradual process of mutual adjustment which will place the sexes on a basis of equilibrium in which each is aware of – and respects and understands – that difference proverbially implied in the Frenchman's cry of '*Vive la différence!*'

MAILER

This country's entering into the most desperate, nightmarish time in its history. Unless everyone in America gets a great deal braver, everything is going to get worse, including the womanization of America.

THE ART OF FICTION:
A *Paris Review* Interview

What writers have you learned the most from, technically?

E. M. Forster, I suppose. I wouldn't say he is necessarily one of the novelists I admire most. But I have learned a lot from him. You remember in *The Longest Journey* somewhere about the fourth chapter, you turn the page and read, 'Gerald was killed that day. He was beaten to death in a football game.' It was quite extraordinary. Gerald had been very important through the beginning of the book. But now that he was suddenly and abruptly dead, everyone else's character began to shift. It taught me that personality was more fluid, more dramatic and startling, more inexact than I had thought. I was brought up on the idea that when you wrote a novel you tried to build a character who could be handled and walked around like a piece of sculpture. Suddenly character seemed related more closely to the paintings of the new realists. For instance I saw one recently which had a painted girl reclining on a painted bed, and there was a television set next to her in the canvas, a real one which you could turn on. Turning on the literal factual set changes the girl and the painting both. Well, Forster gives you something of that sensation in his novels. I suppose what I realized, after reading Forster, was that a novel written in the third person was now impossible for me for many years.

Forster has never written a novel in the first person.

MAILER

I know he hasn't, but in some funny way Forster gave my notion of personality a sufficient shock that I could not manage to write in the third person. Forster, after all, had a developed view of the world. I did not. I think I must have felt at that time as if I would never be able to write in the third person until I developed a coherent view of life. I don't know that I've been able to altogether.

INTERVIEWER

Would you say something about style, prose style, in relation to the novel?

MAILER

A really good style comes only when a man has become as good as he can be. Style is character. A good style cannot come from a bad undisciplined character. Now a man may be evil, but I believe that people can be evil in their essential natures and still have good characters. Good in the sense of being well tuned. They can have characters which are flexible, supple, adaptable, principled in relation to their own good or their own evil – even an evil man can have principles; he can be true to his own evil, which is not always so easy, either. I think good style is a matter of rendering out of oneself all the cupidities, all the cripplings, all the velleities. And then I think one has to develop one's physical grace. Writers who are possessed of some physical grace may tend to write better than writers who are physically clumsy. It's my impression this is so.

INTERVIEWER

Have you ever written to merely improve your writing, practiced your writing as an athlete would work out?

MAILER

No. I don't think it's a proper activity. That's too much like doing a setting-up exercise; any workout which does not involve a certain minimum of danger or responsibility does not improve the body – it just wears it out.

INTERVIEWER

In writing your novels, has any particular formal problem given you trouble – let's say a problem of joining two parts of a narrative together, getting people from point *A* to point *B*?

MAILER

You mean like getting them out of a room? I think formal problems exist in inverse proportion to one's honesty. You get to the problem of getting someone out of the room when there's something false about the scene.

INTERVIEWER

Have you ever written about a situation of which you have had no personal experience or knowledge?

MAILER

I don't know. Let's see . . . *Barbary Shore,* for example, is the most imaginative of my novels. But I did live in a rooming house for a short period while I was writing *The Naked and the Dead.* I certainly didn't live in it the way my characters lived in it. I never met an F.B.I. agent, at least I had no sense of having met one at the time I was writing *Barbary Shore.* They didn't necessarily introduce themselves to me. I had never met an Old Bolshevik, either. But notice this! Writing about F.B.I. agents and Old Bolsheviks in *Barbary Shore,* the greatest single difficulty with the book was that my common sense thought it was impossible to have all these agents and impossible heroes congregating in a rooming house in Brooklyn Heights. Yet a couple of years later I was working in a studio on Fulton Street at the end of Brooklyn Heights, a studio I have had for some years. It was a fine old studio building and they're tearing it down now to make room for a twenty-story building which will look like a Kleenex box. At any rate, on the floor below me, worked one Colonel Rudolph Abel who was the most important spy for the Russians in this country for a period of about eight or ten years, and I am sure we used to be in the elevator together many times. I think he literally had the room beneath me. I have always been overcome with that. It made me decide there's no clear boundary between experience and imagination. Who knows what glimpses of reality we pick up unconsciously, telepathically.

INTERVIEWER

To what extent are your characters modeled on real people?

MAILER

I think half of them might have a point of departure from somebody real. Up to now I've not liked writing about people who are close to me, because they're too difficult to do. Their private reality obviously interferes with the reality one is trying to create. They become alive not as creatures in your imagination but as actors in your life. And so they seem real while you work but you're not working *their* reality into your book. For example it's not a good idea to try to put your wife into a novel. Not your latest wife, anyway. In practice I prefer to draw a character from someone I hardly know.

INTERVIEWER

Can you describe how you turn a real person into a fictional one?

MAILER

I try to put the model in situations which have very little to do with his real situations in life. Very quickly the model disappears. His private reality can't hold up. For instance, I might take somebody who is a professional football player, a man let's say whom I know slightly, and make him a movie star. In a transposition of this sort, everything which relates particularly to the professional football player quickly disappears, and what is left, curiously, is what is *exportable* in his character. But this process while interesting in the early stages is not as exciting as the more creative act of allowing your characters to grow once they're separated from the model. It's when they become almost as complex as one's own personality that the fine excitement begins. Because then they are not really characters any longer – they're beings, which is a distinction I like to make. A character is someone you can grasp as a whole, you can have a clear idea of him, but a being is someone whose nature keeps shifting. Like a character of Forster's. In *The Deer Park* Lulu Meyers is a being rather than a character. If you study her closely you will see that she is a different person in every scene. Just a little different. I don't know whether initially I did this by accident or purposefully, but at a certain point I made the conscious decision *not* to try to straighten her out; she seemed right in her changeableness.

INTERVIEWER

Is Marion Faye a character or a—

MAILER

No, he's a being. Everybody in *The Deer Park* is a being except the minor characters like Herman Teppis.

INTERVIEWER

How did Marion Faye emerge?

MAILER

The book needed something which wasn't in the first draft, some sort of evil genius. One felt a dark pressure there in the inner horizon of the book. But even as I say this I know it's not true to the grain of my writing experience. I violate that experience by talking in these terms. I am not sure it's possible to describe the experience of novel writing authentically. It may be that it is not an experience.

INTERVIEWER

What is it, then?

MAILER

It may be more like a relation, if you will – a continuing relation between a man and his wife. You can't necessarily speak of that as an experience because it may consist of several experiences which are braided together; or it may consist of many experiences which are all more or less similar, or indeed it may consist of two kinds of experiences which are antagonistic to one another. Throughout all of this I've spoken of characters *emerging*. Quite often they don't emerge; they fail to emerge. And what one's left with is the dull compromise which derives from two kinds of experiences warring with one another within oneself. A character who should have been brilliant is dull. Or even if a character does prove to be first-rate, it's possible you should have done twice as much with him, three times as much.

INTERVIEWER

You speak of character as emerging, and I gather by that that you mean emerging from yourself and emerging from your idea?

MAILER

They are also emerging from the book. A book takes on its own life in the writing. It has its laws, it becomes a creature to you after a while. One feels a bit like a master who's got a fine animal. Very often I'll feel a certain shame for what I've done with a novel. I won't say it's the novel that's bad; I'll say it's I who was bad. Almost as if the novel did not really belong to me, as if it was something raised by me like a child. I know what's potentially beautiful in my novel, you see. Very often after I've done the novel I realize that that beauty which I recognize in it is not going to be recognized by the reader. I didn't succeed in bringing it out. It's very odd – it's as though I had let the novel down, owed it a duty which I didn't fulfill.

CAC–F

INTERVIEWER

Would you say that there was any secret or hidden pattern being worked out in your novels?

MAILER

I'd rather leave that to others. If I answer the question badly, nothing is accomplished. If I answer too well, it's going to discourage critics. I can imagine nothing more distressing to a critic than to have a writer see accurately into his own work. But I will say one thing, which is that I have some obsession with how God exists. Is He an essential god or an existential god; is He all-powerful or is He, too, an embattled existential creature who may succeed or fail in His vision? I think this theme may become more apparent as the novels go on.

INTERVIEWER

When did this obsession begin?

MAILER

I think it began to show itself while I was doing the last draft of *The Deer Park*. Then it continued to grow as a private theme during all the years I was smoking marijuana.

INTERVIEWER

You have spoken so often of the existential view. What reading, or individuals, brought you to this?

MAILER

The experience came first. One's condition on marijuana is always existential. One can feel the importance of each moment and how it is changing one. One feels one's being, one becomes aware of the enormous apparatus of nothingness – the hum of a hi-fi set, the emptiness of a pointless interruption, one becomes aware of the war between each of us, how the nothingness in each of us seeks to attack the being of others, how our being in turn is attacked by the nothingness in others. I'm not speaking now of violence or the active conflict between one being and another. That still belongs to drama. But the war between being and nothingness is the underlying illness of the twentieth century. Boredom slays more of existence than war.

INTERVIEWER

Then you didn't come to existentialism because it was a literary influence?

MAILER

No. I'd hardly read anything by Sartre at this time, and nothing by Heidegger. I've read a bit since, and have to admire their formidable powers, but I suspect they are no closer to the buried continent of existentialism than were medieval cartographers near to a useful map of the world. The new continent which shows on our psychic maps as intimations of eternity is still to be discovered.

INTERVIEWER

What do you feel about the other kinds of writing you have done and are doing? How do they stand in relation to your work as a novelist?

MAILER

The essays?

INTERVIEWER

Yes: journalism, essays.

MAILER

Well, you know, there was a time when I wanted very much to belong to the literary world. I wanted to be respected the way someone like Katherine Anne Porter used to be respected.

INTERVIEWER

How do you think she was respected?

MAILER

The way a cardinal is respected – weak people get to their knees when the cardinal goes by.

INTERVIEWER

As a master of the craft, do you mean?

MAILER

As a master of the craft, yes. Her name is invoked in an argument. 'Well, Katherine Anne Porter would not do it *that* way.' But by now I'm a bit cynical about craft. I think there's a natural mystique in the novel which is more important than craft. One is trying, after all, to capture reality, and that is extraordinarily and exceptionally difficult. I think craft is merely a series of waystations. I think of craft as being like a St Bernard dog with that little bottle of brandy under his neck. Whenever you get into *real* trouble the thing that can save you as a novelist is to have enough craft to be able to keep warm long enough to be rescued. Of course this is exactly what keeps good novelists from becoming great novelists. Robert Penn Warren might have written a major novel if he hadn't had just that little extra bit of craft to get him out of all the trouble in *All the King's Men*. If Penn Warren hadn't known anything about Elizabethan literature, the true Elizabethan in him might have emerged. I mean, he might have written a fantastic novel. As it was, he knew enough about craft to . . .

INTERVIEWER

To use it as an escape hatch?

MAILER

Yes. And his plot degenerated into a slam-bang of exits and entrances, confrontations, tragedies, quick wits and woe. But he was really forcing an escape from the problem.

INTERVIEWER

Which was?

MAILER

Oh, the terror of confronting a reality which might open into more and more anxiety and so present a deeper and deeper view of the abyss. Craft protects one from facing those endless expanding realities of deterioration and responsibility.

INTERVIEWER

Deterioration in what sense?

MAILER

The terror, let's say, of being reborn as something much less noble or something much more ignoble. I think this sort of terror depresses us profoundly. Which may be why we throw up our enormous evasions – such as craft. Indeed, I think this adoration of craft, this specific respect for craft makes a church of literature for that vast number of writers who are somewhere on the spectrum between mediocrity and talent. But I think it's fatal for somebody who has a large ambition and a chance of becoming a great writer. I know for myself, if I am going to make this attempt, that the only way to do it is to keep in shape in a peculiar way.

INTERVIEWER

Can you explain what you mean by that?

MAILER

It's hard to talk about. Harry Greb, for example, was a fighter who used to keep in shape. He was completely a fighter, the way one might wish to be completely a writer. He always did the things which were necessary to him as a fighter. Now, some of these things are extremely irrational, that is, extremely irrational from a prize-fight manager's point of view. That is, before he had a fight he would go to a brothel, and he would have two prostitutes, not one, taking the two of them into the same bed. And this apparently left him feeling like a wild animal. Don't ask me why. Perhaps he picked the two meanest whores in the joint and so absorbed into his system all the small, nasty, concentrated evils which had accumulated from carloads of men. Greb was known as the dirtiest fighter of his time. He didn't have much of a punch but he could spoil other fighters and punish them, he knew more dirty tricks than anyone around. This was one of his training methods and he did it over and over again until he died at a relatively early age of a heart attack, on an operating table. I think he died before he was thirty-eight, or so. They operated on him, and bang, he went. Nothing could be done. But the point I make is that he stayed in training by the way he lived his life. The element which was paramount in it was to keep in shape. If he was drinking, you see, the point was to keep in shape *while* drinking. I'm being a touch imprecise about this ...

INTERVIEWER

Well ... what?

MAILER

He would not just drink to release his tension. Rather, what went on was that there was tension in him which was insupportable, so he had to drink. But reasoning as a professional he felt that if he had to drink, he might as well use that too. In the sense that the actor uses everything which happens to him, so Greb as a fighter used everything which happened to him. As he drank he would notice the way his body moved. One of the best reasons one drinks is to become aware of the way his mind and body move.

INTERVIEWER

Well, how do you keep in shape?

MAILER

Look, before we go on, I want to say a little more about craft. It is a grab bag of procedures, tricks, lore, formal gymnastics, symbolic superstructures, methodology in short. It's the compendium of what you've acquired from others. And since great writers communicate a vision of existence, one can't usually borrow their methods. The method is married to the vision. No, one acquires craft more from good writers and mediocre writers with a flair. Craft after all is what you can take out whole from their work. But keeping in shape is something else. For example, you can do journalism, and it can be terrible for your style. Or it can temper your style ... in other words you can become a *better* writer by doing a lot of different kinds of writing. Or you can deteriorate. There's a book came out a few years ago which was a sociological study of some Princeton men – I forget the name of it. One of them said something which I thought was extraordinary. He said he wanted to perform the sexual act under every variety of condition, emotion, and mood available to him. I was struck with this not because I ever wanted necessarily to have that kind of sexual life, but because it seemed to me that was what I was trying to do with my writing. I try to go over my work in every conceivable mood. I edit on a spectrum which runs from the high clear manic impressions of a drunk which has made one electrically alert all the way down to the soberest reaches of depression where I can hardly bear my words. By the time I'm done with writing I care about I usually have worked on it through the full gamut of my consciousness. If you keep yourself in this peculiar kind of shape, the craft will take care of itself. Craft is very little finally. But if you're continually worrying about whether you're growing or deteriorating as a man, whether your integrity is turning soft or firming itself, why then it's in that slow war, that slow rear-guard battle you fight against diminishing talent that you stay in shape as a writer and have a consciousness. You develop a consciousness as you grow older which enables you to write about anything, in effect, and write about it well. That is, provided you keep your consciousness in shape and don't relax into the flabby styles of thought which surround one everywhere. The moment you borrow other writers' styles of thought, you need craft to shore up the walls. But if what you write is a reflection of your own consciousness, then even journalism can become interesting. One wouldn't want to spend one's life at it and I wouldn't want ever to be caught justifying journalism as a major activity (it's obviously less interesting than to write a novel), but it's better, I think, to see journalism as a venture of one's ability to keep in shape, than to see it as an essential betrayal of the chalice of your literary art. Temples are for women.

INTERVIEWER

Temples are for women?

MAILER

Temples are for women.

INTERVIEWER

Well, Faulkner once said that nothing can injure a man's writing if he's a first-rate writer.

MAILER

Faulkner said more asinine things than any other major American writer. I can't remember a single interesting remark Faulkner ever made.

INTERVIEWER

He once called Henry James a 'nice old lady'.

MAILER

Faulkner had a mean small Southern streak in him, and most of his pronunciamentos reflect that meanness. He's a great writer, but he's not at all interesting in most of his passing remarks.

INTERVIEWER

Well, then, what can ruin a first-rate writer?

MAILER

Booze, pot, too much sex, too much failure in one's private life, too much attrition, too much recognition, too little recognition, frustration. Nearly everything in the scheme of things works to dull a first-rate talent. But the worst probably is cowardice – as one gets older, one becomes aware of one's cowardice, the desire to be bold which once was a joy gets heavy with caution and duty.

INTERVIEWER

What kind of an audience do you keep in mind when you write?

MAILER

I suppose it's that audience which has no tradition by which to measure their experience but the intensity and clarity of their inner lives. That's the audience I'd like to be good enough to write for.

INTERVIEWER

Do you feel under any obligation to them?

MAILER

Yes. I have a consciousness now which I think is of use to them. I've got to be able to get it out and do it well, to transmit it in such a way that their experience can rise to a higher level. It's exactly – I mean, one doesn't want one's children to make one's own mistakes. Let them make better mistakes, more exceptional mistakes.

INTERVIEWER

What projects do you have for the future?

MAILER

I've got a very long novel I want to do. And beyond that I haven't looked.

INTERVIEWER

You once said you wished to become consecutively more disruptive, more dangerous, and more powerful, and you felt this sentence was a description of your function as a novelist. I wonder if you still think that?

MAILER

I might take out 'disruptive'. It's an unhappy word to use. It implies a love of disruption for the sake of disruption. Actually, I have a fondness for order.

INTERVIEWER

Do you enjoy writing, or is such a term irrelevant to your experience?

MAILER

Oh no. No, no. You set me thinking of something Jean Malaquais once said. He always has a terrible time writing. He once complained with great anguish about the unspeakable difficulties he was having with a novel. And I asked him, 'Why do you do it? You can do many other things well. Why do you bother with it?' I really meant this. Because he suffered when writing like no one I know. He looked up in surprise and said, 'Oh, but this is the only way one can ever find the truth. The only time I know that something is true is at the moment I discover it in the act of writing.' I think it's that. I think it's this moment of intellection, this moment of seizure when one knows it's true. One may not have written it well enough for others to know, but you're in love with the truth when you discover it at the point of a pencil. That in and by itself is one of the few rare pleasures in life.

INTERVIEWER

And to be writing – to be a writer?

MAILER

Well, at best you affect the consciousness of your time, and so indirectly you affect the history of the time which succeeds you. Of course, you need patience. It takes a long time for sentiments to collect into an action, and often they never do. Which is why I was once so ready to conceive of running for Mayor of New York. I wanted to make actions rather than effect sentiments. But I've come to the middle-aged conclusion that I'm probably better as a writer than a man of action. Too bad. Still it's no little matter to be a writer. There's that Godawful *Time* Magazine world out there, and one can make raids on it. There are palaces, and prisons to attack. One can even succeed now and again in blowing holes in the line of the world's communications. Sometimes I feel as if there's a vast guerrilla war going on for the mind of man, communist against communist, capitalist against capitalist, artist against artist. And the stakes are huge. Will we spoil the best secrets of life or will we help to free a new kind of man? It's intoxicating to think of that. There's something rich waiting if one of us is brave enough and good enough to get there.

Our Argument All But Discontinued

A short story follows. Because it is fiction, no comment is called for (other than to satisfy our scheme by remarking that the confrontation is conceivably between a man and some advancing orders of emptiness).

THE KILLER: *A Story*

'Now,' he said to me, 'do you think you're going to bear up under the discipline of parole?'

'Yessir,' I said.

He had white hair even though he was not more than fifty-two. His face was red. He had blue eyes. He was red, white, and blue. It was a fact I noticed before. They had this coloring. Maybe that was why they identified with the nation.

'In effect you're swearing that you won't take a drink for eight months.'

'I know, sir, but I haven't had a drink inside for four years.' Which was a lie. Three times I had come in with my cellmate on part of a bottle. The first time I was sick. The second time we had a fight, a quiet fight which I lost. He banged my head on the floor. Without noise. The third time we had sex. Democratic sex. We did each other.

'You understand that parole is not freedom.'

'Yessir.'

They asked these questions. They always asked the same questions, and they always got the same answers. It had nothing to do with what you said. It had nothing to do with how you shaved or how you combed your hair because you combed your hair the way everybody else did, and the day you went up to Board you shaved twice. Maybe, it had to do with how many shaving cuts you had, but I didn't have any. I had taken care, wow. Suppose it had to do with the way you moved. If two of the three men on the parole board liked the way you moved, you were all right, provided they didn't like the way you moved too much. Sex. No matter who I'm with, man or woman, always get a feeling off them. At least I used to. I always could tell if they were moving inside or moving away, and I could tell if anything was going on inside. If we ever touched, I could tell better. Once I was in a streetcar and a girl sat down next to me. She was a full barrel. A very fat girl. Pretty face. I don't like fat. Very fat people have no quick. They can always stop. They can stop from doing a lot of things.

This girl and me had a future however. Her hip touched. I could feel what I did to her. From side of my leg, through my pants, and her dress, through some kind of corset, cheap plastic corset, something bad, through that, through her panties, right into her, some current went out of me, and I could feel it in her, opening up future. She didn't do a thing, didn't move. Fixed.

Well, five minutes, before I got off at my stop. In those minutes I was occupied by a project with that girl where we projected five years. I knew what I could do to her. I say without exaggeration I could take her weight down from one hundred eighty to one-eighteen in a year and it would have been a pleasure because all that fat was stored-up sugar she was saving. For somebody. She was stingy, congealed like lard, but I had the current to melt that. I knew it would not be hard to pick her up. If I did, the rest would happen. I would spend a year with her. It is difficult to pick up a fat girl, but I would have used shock treatment. For example, I would have coughed, and dropped an oyster on her skirt. I think it is revolting to do something like that, but it would have worked with this fat girl because disgust would have woke her up. That's the kind of dirt sex is, in the mind of somebody fat and soft and clammy. Sex to them is spit and mucus. It would have given me the opportunity to wipe it off. I could trust my fingers to give a touch of something. The point to the entire operation (people watching in the streetcar, me standing with my handkerchief, apologizing) would be that my fingers would be doing two things at once, proper and respectful in the part of my hand everybody else could see, flame through the handkerchief on her lap. I would have begun right there. For the least I would get her name. At the end of the five minutes I turned to take a look at her, and under that fat face, in the pretty face which could be very attractive, I could see there was a dumb look in her eyes that nothing was going to improve. That stopped me. Putting in a year on a girl like that would be bad unless she was all for me at the end. Stupidity is for nothing, not even itself. I detest stupidity in women – it sets me off. So I got off the car. Didn't even look at the girl. After she gets married to somebody fat and stupid like herself she will hate any man who looks like me because of that five minutes. Her plastic corset must have had a drug-store smell after I got off the trolley car. Think of plastic trying to smell.

I tell this as an example. On the outside it used to be that I never sat down next to anybody that I didn't feel them even when we didn't touch and two or three times a week, or even a day, I would be close to the possibilities of somebody like the fat girl. I know about certain things. I know with all policemen, detectives, correction officers, turnkeys, hacks, parole-board officials, that sex is the problem with them. Smartest cellmate I had said one time like a philosopher, 'Why, man, a judge will forgive any crime he is incapable of committing himself.' My friend put it right. Sex is a bitch. With police. They can't keep their hands off. They do, but then it builds tension. For some it's bad. They can get ready to kill. That's why you comb your hair. Why you must look neat. You have to be clean. Above sex. Then a cop can like you. They ask you those questions knowing how you will answer. Often they know you are lying. For example they know that you will take a drink in the next six months. What is important is not that you are lying, but the kind of lie they hear in your voice. Are you afraid of them? Are you afraid they will see down into your lying throat? Then you are okay. They will pass you. If you are afraid of them, you're a good risk. But if you think they are stupid, faintest trace of such a thought in yourself, it comes through. Always one of them will be sensitive to condescension. It gets them ready to kill. A policeman never forgives you when you get him ready to kill. Obviously he can't do it, especially in a room performing official duty with a stenographer at the side. But the adrenalin goes through him. It is bad to take a flush of adrenalin for nothing. All that murder and nowhere to go. For example when you're standing up talking to a parole board it's important the way you stand, how tight your pants are. Good to be slim, trim, shipshape, built the way I am, provided you are modest. Do not project your groin forward or your hips back. It is best if your pants are not tight-fit. Younger juvenile delinquents actually make this sort of mistake. It is not that they are crazy as much as egotistical. They think older men will like them so much they will give them parole in order to look them up. A mistake. Once read in the newspapers about a Russian soldier who picked up a German baby and said, 'It's beautiful,' but then he got angry because he remembered the baby's father had been shooting his children, so he killed the baby. That's a cop. If you strut, even in good taste and subtle, they will start to get a glow where it is verboten, and they will like you, they will get a little rosy until they sense it goes nowhere, and wow the sex turns. Gets ready to kill you. If cops have an adrenalin wash for their trouble, you are remembered badly. It is much better to be slim, trim, shipshape, and a little peaked-looking, so they can see you as a thrifty son, which is the way they must have seen me because they gave parole that day, and I was out of there in a week. Out of prison. Out of the can. I think I would have died another year. Liver sickness or go berserk.

Now you may ask can police be so dumb as to let me go on an armed-robbery sentence, six years unserved out of ten. Well, they saw me as thrifty. I was careful that day with voice and posture. But how can police be so stupid as to think in categories like thrifty? That's easy, I can answer. Police are pent up, they're apes, they're bulls. Bulls think in categories.

2

Well, I've been feeling small for four years now. Prison is a bitch for people like me. It cuts your – I don't want to use doubtful language. It's a habit you build up inside. Some do use language that way. Some lifers. Spades. People who don't give a damn. They're playing prison as if it is their life, the only one they are going to have. But I am conservative in temperament. I comb my hair every morning, I comb it the same way. Minor matter you may say, but it isn't for me. I like to comb my hair when I feel like it. Animal of the woods. I have the suspicion – some would call it superstition – that combing my hair can spoil some good ideas. I would never say this to a hack but why is it not possible that some ideas live in your hair, the way the hair curls. I have very wavy hair when it is left to itself. Whenever I get a haircut, I have the feeling I'm losing possibilities I never got around to taking care of. Put it this way: when I comb my hair, it changes my mood. So naturally I prefer to comb it when I want to. In prison forget that. Comb your hair the same time same way every day. Look the same. If you're smart, keep your mood the same way. No ups. Nor downs. Don't be friendly. Don't be sullen. Don't offer company. Don't keep too quiet. If you stay safe, in the middle, and are the same thing every day you get a good report. The reason I get parole first time out, six years off a ten-year sentence is that I was a model prisoner which means just this: you are the same thing every day. Authorities like you if you are dependable. Be almost boring. I think what it may be about is that any man in authority finds his sleep important to him. People in authority can't stand the night. If you wear a uniform and you go to bed to sleep and a certain prisoner never bothers your dreams, you'll say a good word for him when it comes time to making out reports.

Of course you are not popular. Necessarily. My bunky shakes my hand when I get this good news, but I can see he is not happy in every way. So I complain about details. I am not to possess liquor at home, nor am I to frequent any bar even once, even at Christmas. Moreover, I am not to eat in any restaurant which serves liquor.

'What if you don't drink? But just eat there?'

'I'm not to go into any premises having a liquor license.'

'A restaurant that don't serve liquor is a tearoom or a hash house.'

'Crazy,' I say. I don't like such expressions, but this is perfect to express my sentiments.

'Well, good luck.'

It is possible we are thinking of the same things, which is the three times he got a bottle into the cell and we drank it together. The first time sick, second time we had a fight, third time sex. I remember I almost yelled in pain when my rocks got off, because they wouldn't stop. I was afraid I'd hurt myself. It had been so long. It seemed each time I took liquor something started in me that was different from my normal personality. By normal I mean normal in prison, no more. You wouldn't want a personality like that on the outside any more than you would want to smell like a laundry bag. But so far as inside personality went, I couldn't take liquor and keep the same. So if I started drinking on the secret when outside, I was in trouble. Because my style of personality would try to go back to what it was before, and too many eyes would be on me. My parole officer, people in the neighborhood. The parole board was getting me a job. They just about picked out the room where you lived. They would hear about it even if I didn't get into a rumble when I was drunk. If I kept a bottle in my room, I would have to hide it good. The parole officer has been known to come around and pay a friendly visit which is to say a sneak visit. Who could enjoy the idea of him sniffing the air in my room to see was there liquor on the breeze? If they caught me drinking in the eight months, back I would be sent to here. A gamble, this parole. But I was glad to take it, I needed out. Very much. Because there was a monotony in me. I had been coming in day after day. I didn't have the feeling of a current in me any more, of anything going. I had the feeling if I sat down next to a girl like the fat girl now, and our legs touched, she would move away because there was a blank in me which would pass into her. Something repulsive. There was something bad in me, something very dull. It wasn't in my body, it wasn't even in my mind, it was somewhere. I'm not religious, but it was somewhere. I mean I didn't know if I could keep control or not. Still, I couldn't have done it the other way. Eight more months. I might have flipped. Talking back to a hack, a fight. I'd have lost good time. There is only one nightmare in prison. It's that you don't get out, that you never get out because each time you come close the tension has built up in you so that you have to let it break out, and then your bad time is increased. So it's like being on the wrong escalator.

'Take it slow, take it easy,' said my bunky. 'Eight months goes by if you get yourself some sun.'

'Yeah, I'm going to sleep in the sun,' I said. 'I'm going to drink it.'

'Get a good burn your first day out, ha-ha. Burn the prison crap out of your pores.'

Maybe the sun would burn the dullness away. That's what I was thinking.

PART FOUR : ARENA

Our Argument At Last Presented

Now I will give you a set of equations. They are not math-
ematical, but metaphorical; and therefore full of science. I
repeat: they are equations in the form of metaphor; so they
are full of science. It is just that they are not scientific. For
they are equations composed only of words. I am thus trying
to say my equations are a close description of phenomena
which cannot be measured by a scientist. Yet these obser-
vations are clear enough to say that interruption is shock,
and shock deadens mood, but mood then stirs itself to rouse
a wave. Why? Well, the sum of one's experience might sug-
gest that it is probably in the nature of mood to restore itself
by raising a wave. Of course, if the wave is too vigorous a
response to the shock, new waste may be left behind. But if
the wave is adequate to the impulse which begot it, the wave
can clear the waste away. So we come to the measure of the
absurd, and its enigma: some art movements serve to wash
out the sludge of civilization, some leave us deeper in the pit.
The art of the absurd is here to purify us or to swamp us –
we do not know – suddenly, we are back at the GULF *sign.*
Only now we must recognize that we are confronted by no
less than the invisible church of modern science. No small
matter. Science has built a wall across the route of meta-
phor: poets whine before experts.

The difficulty is that none of us, scientists first, are
equipped to measure the achievements of science. That vast
scientific work of the last fifty years has come most
undeniably out of the collective efforts of the twentieth-
century scientist, but the achievement came also out of the
nineteenth century, the Enlightenment, and the Renaissance.
Who may now measure where the creativity was finest? The
scientists of the last five centuries were the builders of that

foundation from which modern scientists have created a modern science. Only these ancestors may have been more extraordinary men. They were adventurers, rebels, courtiers, painters, diplomats, churchmen. Our scientists are only experts; those of the last decade are dull in person as experts, dull as Janos Salk, they write jargon, their minds are narrow before they are deep. Their knowledge of life is incarcerated.

The huge industrial developments and scientific advances of the twentieth century – the automobile, antibiotics, radium, flight, the structure of the atom, relativity, the quantum theory, psychoanalysis, the atom bomb, the exploration of space – may speak not so much for the genius of the twentieth century as for the genius of the centuries which preceded it. Modern science may prove to be the final poisoned fruit of the rich European tree, and plague may disclose itself as the most characteristic invention of our time. For science was founded originally on metaphor, would go our Argument, and the twentieth century has shipped metaphor to the ghetto of poets. Consider: science began with the poetic impulse to treat metaphor as equal to equation; the search began at that point where a poet looked for a means (which only later became experiment) to measure the accuracy of his metaphor. The natural assumption was that his discovery had been contained in the metaphor, since good metaphor could only originate in the deepest experience of a man; so science still remained attached to poetic vision, and scientific insight derived from culture – it was not the original desire of science to convert nature, rather to reveal it. Faust was still unborn when Aristotle undertook his pioneer observations.

There is a danger in metaphor, however; the danger which is present in poetry: contradictory meanings collect too easily about the core of meaning; unconnected meanings connect themselves. So, science sought a methodology through experiment which would be severe, precise, and able to measure the verity of the insight in the metaphor.

Experiment was conceived to protect the scientific artist from ambiguity.

Experiment, however, proliferated; as the scientist ceased to be a great amateur and became expert, experiment ran amuck, and laboratory men of partial, determined, fanatic brilliance became the scientist's director rather than his assistant. The laboratory evicted the mind; the laboratory declared itself the womb of scientific knowledge; laboratory methodology grew as cumbersome as the labor codes of a theatrical union. Metaphor disappeared.

It was replaced by a rabidity of experiment, a fetichism of experiment. Mediocrity invaded science. Experiment became a faith, experiment replaced the metaphor as a means of inquiry, and technological development pushed far ahead of even the most creative intuition. Penicillin was discovered by accident, as a by-product of experiment – it did not come at the end of a poetic journey of the mind. No, it was an orphan and a bastard. And by similar mass methods were all the other antibiotics uncovered, by observing the bactericidal action of a million molds: those which gave the best laboratory evidence of success were marketed by drug companies. But the root of the success was not comprehended. There was no general theory to point to a particular mold for a specific disease. No metaphor. Metaphor had been replaced by gross assay.

Metaphor. The word has been used generously. Would an example be welcome? The Argument can try to provide it. A modern disease, for example, as it is comprehended in a laboratory, is explained to the laboratory technician, the student, and the layman, as a phenomenon made up of its own pimples, rash, swelling and development, but the disease is not ever presented as a creature – real or metaphorical – a creature which might have an existence separate from its description, even as you and I have an existence which is separate from the fact that we weigh so many pounds and stand so many inches tall. No, the symptom is stripped of its presence. Of course, psychoanalysis made an

*attempt to say that the root of one disease could be similar
to the root of another whose symptoms were different; it
was a way of hinting that the metaphor ought to return.
Such an approach might have wished ultimately to demon-
strate that a malfunction of the liver and an inflammation of
the eyes were both connected to despair at one's position in
society. But psychoanalysis was hungry, and dependent
upon the sciences: like most welfare cases it was therefore
not in a rush for poetry – rather it rushed to advertise the
discovery of each new tranquilizer for each disorder in
emotion. It was anxious to show itself respectable. So psy-
chiatry became pharmacology.*

*Let us, however, try to travel in the other direction, let us
look for an extreme metaphor of disease. Let us suppose
that each specific ill of the body is not so much a dull evil to
be disposed of by any chemical means whatever, but is,
rather, a theatrical production presented by some company
in oneself to some audience in oneself. To the degree then
that our illness is painful, detailed, clear, and with as much
edge as a sharply enunciated voice, the particular disease is a*
success; *the communion of the body* (*the statement sent
from stage to audience*) *is deep, is resonant. The audience
experiences catharsis – at the end of the drama, the body is
tired but enriched. By the logic of our metaphor, that is a
good disease. The illness has waged conflict, drama, and dis-
tress through the body, and has obliged the body to sit in
attention upon it, but now the body knows more. Its experi-
ence has become more profound, its intimate knowledge of
its own disharmony is more acute.*

By this reckoning, a disease is the last attempt (at a par-
ticular level of urgency) *to communicate from one part of
the body to the other, a last attempt to tell us that if we do
not realize the function before us is now grievously out of
harmony, then we will certainly sicken further. On the other
hand, if the disease which presents itself is not accepted, if
one's suffering is not suffered, if there are no statements of
our suffering enunciated through the caverns of the body,*

but if instead our disease is averted by antibiotic, or our pain is silenced by a sedative, then the attempted communication of the illness has failed. The disease having no other expression, sinks, of necessity, into a lower and less elegant condition, it retreats from a particular pain or conflict into a bog of disharmony. Where one organ or two might have borne the original stress, now ten organs share ubiquitous tension. A clear sense of symptom tends to disappear. Infection begins to be replaced by virus, a way of saying the new diseases are not classifiable — their symptoms reveal no characteristic form. One is close to the plague.

If my metaphor is valid, then drugs to relieve pain, and antibiotics to kill infection, are invalid. They are in fact liquidators of possibility, for they deaden the possibility of any quick dramatic growth. A disease checked by an antibiotic has taught the body nothing — nothing to terminate ambiguity — for the body does not know how well it could have cured itself, or even precisely what it had to cure. Yet ambiguity is the seat of disease. Ambiguity demands double communication to achieve a single purpose. It demands we be ready for a particular course of action and yet be ready for its exact opposite. So it demands double readiness or double function for single use. Ambiguity is therefore waste. A man brought back from death by chemicals his own body did not manage to provide cannot know afterward if he should be alive. Small matter, you may argue; he is much alive, is he not? But he has lost biological dignity, he is crucially less alive in a part of his mind and his body. That is one reason metaphors are not encouraged near to science now, for one would then have to say that the patient is alive, but his soul has died a degree.

So the Argument would demand that there be metaphors to fit the vaults of modern experience. That is, in fact, the unendurable demand of the middle of this century, to restore the metaphor, and thereby displace the scientist from his center. Would you call for another example? Think of the elaborate architecture in the structure of a protein molecule. The scientist will describe the structure and list the properties of the molecule (and indeed it took technological achievements close to genius to reach that point) but the scientist will not look at the metaphorical meaning of the physical structure, its meaning as an architectural form. He will not ponder what biological or spiritual experience is suggested by the formal structure of the molecule, for metaphor is not to the present interest of science. It is instead the desire of science to be able to find the cause of cancer in some virus: a virus – you may count on it – which will be without metaphor. You see, that will then be equal to saying that the heart of the disease of all diseases is empty of meaning, that cancer is caused by a specific virus which has no character or quality, and is in fact void of philosophy and bereft of metaphysics. All those who are there to claim that disease and death are void of meaning are there to benefit from such a virus, for next they can move on to say that life is absurd. We are back once again at the enigma surrounding the art of the absurd. Except now we have hints of the meaning. For if the Argument would propose that a future to life depends on creating forms of an intensity which will capture the complexity of modern experience and dignify it, illumine – if you will – its danger, then the art of the absurd reveals the wound in its own heart and the schizophrenia of its impulse, for the art of the absurd wars with one hand against the monotonies of all totalitarian form in politics, medicine, architecture, and media communication, and with the other, trembles and is numb to any human passion and is savage toward discourse, for the danger is palpable and the discovery of new meaning may live in ambush at the center of a primitive fire.

Well, enough of such metaphor. Let us go off to explore the tributaries of form.

The Political Economy of Time

MAILER

We have had an agreeable dialogue until now. It has been superficial in all too many places, and the reasonings have been limited finally by my ability to reason, which is famously limited, but our subject matter proved rich. Feces, after all, are first cousin to gold. If we were obliged to talk of death, there was at least a sense of blood. But today we're off on emptier matters – out in the vacuums of metaphysics, and I have slept poorly, and dreamed of barren landscapes, empty beach, and stagnant pools on a winter day. There will be the taste of this in what we talk of next.

INTERVIEWER

Your mind is dull, you say.

MAILER

It is overstimulated and next to empty. I've had too much coffee, and excitation put upon depression seems to produce an excess of electric in the nerve.

INTERVIEWER

You advance this metaphor as the secret of everything electric?

MAILER

I steal away from it.

INTERVIEWER

Good. Because we are here to talk about form; and electricity, I suspect, has no form, only property.

MAILER

(*In gloom*) We are here to talk about form.

INTERVIEWER

Make then a formal beginning.

MAILER

Instead let me start by paying my respects to an irony. It is that some fundamental subjects are easy to discuss. The word 'soul', for example, lends itself to speculation. But 'form!' There's a treacherous word. It can mean the opposite of itself.

INTERVIEWER

To me, form is an easy word. I think I understand it.

MAILER

You do?

INTERVIEWER

Form always means the shape of something.

MAILER

(*Shows a fraction of interest*) The form of an umbrella is the shape of the umbrella?

INTERVIEWER

Absolutely. That's all there is to it. An umbrella has a form which is identical to its shape. (*Interviewer stops*) Actually, I must admit that, in fact, it has two shapes. Its shape when it is open, and its shape when it is closed.

MAILER

Then it has two forms?

INTERVIEWER

Yes.

MAILER

What about a tree?

INTERVIEWER

(*Takes his time*) A tree has a form which is its own form, its own particular form. But I see what you are driving at. It also has a form which is the form of all trees of its species.

MAILER

These two forms of the tree are different from the two forms of the umbrella? That is – we are speaking of different kinds of categories?

INTERVIEWER

I think we are.

MAILER

Consider this: what is the form of an amoeba?

INTERVIEWER

An amoeba has no form. It's shapeless.

MAILER

Modern coffee tables are cut into what is presumably a shape called amoeboid.

INTERVIEWER

(*His confidence is back*) The word means no more than that an object is presented in meaningless curves. It does not mean an amoeba has shape. Take the two forms of the tree. Can't I say that not only does the amoeba not have an individual shape, and so not have a particular form which is like the first form of the tree (that is to say, its form at a given moment) but that all amoebac taken as a class do not possess a general shape, a secondary group shape we might call amoeboid, a shape that would be like the second form of the tree.

MAILER

The fact remains: the amoeba may have a shape at any instant.

INTERVIEWER

(*Full of momentum*) Not if it changes constantly. If it keeps changing, the amoeba can have a shape only if you insist on picking a moment when you freeze time. Very much against time's own will, if I may speak that way. A microphotograph would give the amoeba a shape. But only arbitrarily. A concept like the differential of time, *dt*, in calculus might be able to give it a shape. But those are stage tricks. If the amoeba keeps changing, it cannot possess a particular shape.

MAILER

Suppose when examined closely, the amoeba moves for an instant, is still, then moves again? Can't we select each moment it is at rest and call that a particular shape?

INTERVIEWER

Suppose the amoeba is never completely at rest?

MAILER

Then there is no *particular* form. A *particular* form cannot be detected without a moment of rest. But that should not keep the amoeba from possessing an ideal form.

INTERVIEWER

An ideal form? You speak of the second kind of form? Like the second form of the tree? The form which is the form of all trees?

MAILER

Yes. A man, for example, might possess an ideal form. We could say his ideal form remains unchanged whether he is running, walking, or sleeping. That is because when we speak of his ideal form, we are speaking of a shape he can *probably* assume. (Of course he may have to go on a diet to demonstrate it.) But note that it is not his particular shape until he assumes it.

INTERVIEWER

I can agree with that.

MAILER

Now the amoeba may not possess such an abstract ideal form. I have no idea if it does. But whether it owns an ideal form or not seems to me on reflection not to the point. I wish you only to agree that the amoeba, hypothetically, may have a set of consecutive shapes as discernible as the successive frames of a movie film.

INTERVIEWER

We come back to the problem of rest. Why should I concede to you that the amoeba may have a consecutive set of particular shapes if you have not yet demonstrated that it can ever be discovered at rest? All of it – at rest – all at once.

MAILER

Perhaps I can never demonstrate it to you at rest. Perhaps you can demonstrate that it is *never* at rest. You cannot. Will you concede that the amoeba *may* have a set of consecutive shapes?

INTERVIEWER

It may. I still have the feeling it does not have a form. If it's not shapeless, the amoeba is next to shapeless. Because nothing in it seems to remain the same.

MAILER

You demand of form that it have not only shape but security. It must last?

INTERVIEWER

Yes. It must have a shape in time.

MAILER

So it seems we are talking about time as well. About shape and time. Can you then agree that when we speak of form, we are talking of more than shape?

INTERVIEWER

Maybe we are.

MAILER

Would you concede the likelihood that shape is not equal to form, but merely a first best clue to it?

INTERVIEWER

I may have to. But go on.

MAILER

That is, shape is a clue to form if you can see the shape.

INTERVIEWER

I knew I should concede nothing. What has a form you cannot see?

MAILER

Would you permit a symphony to have form?

INTERVIEWER

It must. I see what you're up to. Of course. The sounds we hear in a symphony vary each instant. Only when it's done do we remember the successive sounds as a shape. A shape composed of many sounds heard in a period of time. (*Stops*) I know you may think I am playing with the word, but I believe it is fair to speak of the shape of a piece of music. In my memory, it has not only permanence but a shape.

MAILER

Already you are talking of form in space, and form in time, of forms we see, forms we hear? You see why I did not wish to get impaled on the amoeba at rest?

INTERVIEWER

I see why exactly. And I still say permanence is the first feature of form.

MAILER

Let us say it is a feature of many forms which exist in space or in time. But can't we speak of forms which exist in other conditions?

INTERVIEWER

I should think form can only have a shape in space or time. What else is relevant here?

MAILER

Can taste have form?

INTERVIEWER

. . .

MAILER

Or smell? Or touch? Can they have form?

INTERVIEWER

I don't see how.

MAILER

Could you say the taste of wine is a form?

INTERVIEWER

You're leading me to some borderland of the concepts.

MAILER

To what?

INTERVIEWER

To forms which might exist in being. In Being! You bring in Being because you're an existentialist. Dammit all to hell.

MAILER

I'm thinking of a famous wine. Château Margaux '47. Each time one drinks, the taste comes upon the palate in clear acts. Sweet, cool, then earthy and sad, sweet and cool, earthy, sad. If one drinks too much, the sorrow turns to rust. Such wine has a shape in time. The permanence of its form resides in my memory.

INTERVIEWER

You are trying to connect form to Being. Perhaps you even succeed. To some slight degree. I distrust your motive. You wish to return to a discussion of the soul. So you are trying to smuggle form over into Being.

MAILER

In order to smuggle Being over to soul?

INTERVIEWER

That might be your route. I would remind you that we are far from done with the amoeba and the tree. I started this discussion by remarking that form was the shape of something. Since an amoeba had no consistent shape, it could have no form. You then pointed out that the amoeba's movement contained hypothetical instants of rest, and so one could speak of a possible succession of forms. But I still say the amoeba does not have a permanent shape in time. It is the opposite of a tree. Precisely because a tree has a shape to which you can return in your mind. An ideal shape which is related to an ideal form. There you are! Ideal form suggests permanence. Everything to do with form speaks of permanence.

MAILER

I now propose to demonstrate that ideal form is a treacherous hypothesis. Follow me. There is a kind of form which appears to have a durable shape in time as well as in space. This form you presume is there for the tree. Ideal form, you call it. But there is another kind of visual form which has no shape in any kind of time we can perceive. The amoeba, for example. This lack of shape is perceived as lack-of-shape because we are using man as the measure of time. Only because of that. If we dispense with ourselves as the measure, then I think I can show that the amoeba has a shape which is conceivably definite or indefinite, just as ideal or not ideal, as permanent or impermanent as the shape belonging to the tree.

INTERVIEWER

Let us see you make such a demonstration.

MAILER

To us, a tree changes slowly. Its shape in time alters imperceptibly. But if we take a movie of the tree, if we mount a camera on the wall of a garden during the first season the tree is planted and proceed for the next hundred years (which for simple calculation we may suppose to be the life of the tree) to click off no more than one single frame of film each separate week, we might end with fifty-two hundred frames of film for a century, which by all lightnings of calculation is less than four minutes of projection. In the finished movie our tree would pass through a year in two and a half seconds. Its trunk would sprout and climb toward the sky, its branches would open as fast as an umbrella, the change of color in its leaves from green to red to brown would be a flicker the eye could barely detect. The action of the tree would look spasmodic, convulsive, near to spastic. It might be even reminiscent of the shift of shape in the amoeba.

INTERVIEWER

Still, the tree moves out of a logic which suggests a kind of shape in time. One can see it rise, bud, leaf, lose its leaves, bud again, and go on through a hundred cycles of the years until its death.

MAILER

If the tree were situated in a windless space, one might see that. But assume a small breeze blows the branches one way this week, and the other the next. Then the movements of the tree would have no apparent purpose in our film. Tree limbs would thrash like cilia in a paramecium; the branches would not even possess an outline, but would seem to offer some indefinite nebulous transparent edge.

INTERVIEWER

That is because you film one frame a week. The tiny segments of time you record are unrelated to one another.

MAILER

Only in part are they unrelated. The filmed movement of the branches may be relatively arbitrary, but the film is obedient to the general growth of the trunk and the limbs.

INTERVIEWER

I insist you are being more arbitrary in the way you look at the tree than the way you look at the amoeba.

MAILER

It may be that every procedure we have for looking at anything not human is arbitrary. That is an inhuman remark. Still, I must ask you to conceive of a being on some distant star, some cosmic giant who lives in another rhythm or scale of time, in some relation to time altogether different from ours. A wink of his eyelash occupies a year for us; to him, it is just a wink (that is to say, his personal subjective impression of the duration of his wink is approximately equal to our impression of the duration of our wink). If we close our eye and open it, we have the sensation that a small but definite interval of time has elapsed, something like a second. The giant also feels as if no more than a second has passed, but he is large, his proportions are huge; in fact a year by our measure has passed. Think then of what he might see through some telescope worthy of his size when he studies a tree on earth. It must appear to him as fantastic, nervous, illogical, rapid and shapeless as an amoeba. More so. The life cycle of the tree might look perhaps like a doll or a ballerina who rises from a crouch, shivers, pirouettes and collapses in ninety seconds.

INTERVIEWER

You do not even beg the question, you violate it. What right have you to give this giant another scale of time than ours?

MAILER

I have no right. Neither of us has rights in a discussion of time. Nobody knows anything about time. Consider – what right have you to assume that time is equal anywhere? That its measure is a clock? My notion of time is as reasonable as yours. I use the giant, you use the clock. With the clock, certain kinds of time have to be measured in numbers so great that man is run off the stage and we speak of light-years. I think it is more agreeable to measure time by beings.

INTERVIEWER

What then measures time in each separate being? Soul?

MAILER

Soul.

INTERVIEWER

The amoeba has a soul?

MAILER

Yes.

INTERVIEWER

The tree?

MAILER

Yes.

INTERVIEWER

And their measure of time is proportionate to the relative size?

MAILER

One might say it is probably not unrelated. It seems reasonable to assume that a short interval for the tree might seem like a larger one for the amoeba.

INTERVIEWER

Man and the tree, however, are relatively near to each other in their measure of time?

MAILER

Not necessarily. The condition of Being is so different for each. The hundred years of life a tree can know might seem not nearly enough, a month perhaps to it.

INTERVIEWER

There is a clock in nature. We call it night and day. The tree shares night and day, dark and light with each of us. So does the amoeba in the pond.

MAILER

They do, but they do not necessarily do it in the same way. What is a day for us may be no more than an inhalation of breath for the tree; as we sleep through the night so the tree exhales its breath, the way we might exhale breath as we blink our eyes.

INTERVIEWER

And the amoeba?

MAILER

A day might seem a century in the soul of an amoeba; the night an entombment worthy of Pharaohs. As we look through the microscope we see two tentacles reach out from the amoeba and encircle a morsel. Snap! The morsel is whipped toward the nucleus. Half a second by the clock, or five seconds, or three minutes required. But as we study the amoeba in the field of the microscope, our vision distorted by glass, reflected light, optical ache and biological concept, we may be not unlike my slumbering giant. He sees the tree through a telescope which spans heavens. What adventures and distortions in the air and light! The atmospheres of planets, the echo of meteors, and huge seas of radiation twist his comprehension of the tree. So do the concepts of his gigantic mind. His fingers exhaust our decade in the time it takes him to light a cigarette. His concepts involve actions which take centuries, millenniums, some dull eons. So he cannot conceive the sweet complexity of a day or month for us. Men or trees are a flicker in his lens. His concept of time, his feeling for time's duration, exists in him only by what is suitable to his measure – which is gargantuan, not human, so that he misses everything of human scale just as we are all but closed off from the gargantuan. Look! Man has a decent sense of the hours, the minutes, the days, the years, the seasons, the decades, the instants, the lifetimes, the moments and the centuries. For these he has built a clock. But for the light-years or the micromillionth of a second he has no clock. There, his sense of time is blind. Man's clock becomes absurd. Light-years or micromillionths of a second are categories of time outside the proportions of our life, or our situation in the universe. A being like you or me can comprehend any unit of time, whether arbitrary and measured like a minute or natural like a moment, if it is at least part of the length of our life, if it is pertinent to what I wish to call our *enlifement* – our subjective or biological conception of the size of time. We can only be sensitive to those proportions of time which are a measure of our life. Conversely, we can only have the confidence to understand the sense of time of beings like ourselves. For this reason, we can have reasonable hope of understanding such creations as man. But a being which exists in a radically different enlifement, a being like an amoeba, or like a tree, will have a different measure. *Snap!* go the tentacles of the amoeba. Just three seconds taken. But for the amoeba, those three seconds may have been a convocation of events as complex as the movements of a modern army – those three seconds could have been a year's campaign in the mud, and the particle of food as differentiated and as dangerous as an enemy force. Its form might have been exceptional if we had proper eyes and concepts which is to say if we lived in the very amoeboid time necessary to glimpse what had been before the amoeba.

INTERVIEWER

Don't you exaggerate? May it be not just an amoeba? Nothing going on but a little wiggle to snap up some food?

MAILER

My cosmic giant might have been able to see the German armies surrounded at Stalingrad. Without his telescope, however, the battle could have looked to him no more impressive than one of those larger amoebae, half the size of the head of a pin, which one can sometimes see on the surface of a pollen in a quiet pond.

INTERVIEWER

Which is a way of saying all of us are insignificant.

MAILER

Maybe it is the giant who is insignificant; maybe it is his emotions which are dim. We may be weak in relation to the power of the giant, but he may be insignificant in his emotions, in his perception. His size could speak for the heroic, or could mean no more than that the giant lost all conception of a future and so chose to proliferate himself into an enormous but sluggish space. The giant might be no more interesting than a million miles of styrene.

INTERVIEWER

Space is the measure of power, you are saying, but time is the index of what is possible.

MAILER

That is possible.

INTERVIEWER

So the amoeba is more glorious than you or me.

MAILER

It may be; maybe it is not. Some amoebae are doubtless glorious, some odious. There may be at this instant wars amoebae are fighting which mean more to the future of our being than all rocket ships. We don't know. The amoeba's lack of size and its tremendous number may signify less than we know.

INTERVIEWER

Their number! There are millions of amoebae for each one of us. Or is it billions? They cannot be individual.

MAILER

What if they are some other kind of being altogether? What if all the amoebae in one freshwater pond constitute no more than one soul, one very special sort of soul, not really a soul if you will, but some element of Being, some spirit of the pond. Postulate more men on earth than ponds. If there is an exceptional creation to each pond—

INTERVIEWER

You cheat. You speak of every amoeba possessing a soul, now you speak of all the amoebae within a pond as one single soul. I think you want to bring the conversation around to some back alley, some purlieu of the soul, where no philosophical rigor can catch up to you.

MAILER

We've come to a point of such fearful complexity that I may as well confess that after our conversations of yesterday I have been up half the night trying to find a way to explain some notions to you. But then I began our conversation with complaints. Still, I wish you would understand that I have no desire to discuss the soul. On the contrary, that opens empty vistas, as if indeed you can use up your soul by talking about it. For one thing, the language is unendurable. You must employ words which have been used by the worst churchmen, wardens, editors, policemen, politicians, generals, statesmen and financiers of each century, just such words as God, soul, Devil, spirit, vision, eternal and universal. It may be possible to bring new connotations to these words, although I doubt it. But the alternative is, after all, worse; it is to make up your own words: call the soul psyche or being-in-itself; the will, ego; the conscience, super-ego; call God the Force of Life or the Being of Being; call the Devil Negation; call eternity a limitless parameter; translate the Vision into transcendental numina. There is nausea in such procedure. So I take the words as they are, talk of soul and spirit. I am, you see, obliged to go on because I can't leave our conversation unfinished here. That alternative is even meaner to contemplate. Yet, if I proceed, understand that I am filled with a sense of discomfort. The continuation will be, I expect, so intangible, changeable, and contradictory that the task of communicating it will be similar in difficulty to taking hold of a spider's web in order to pass on something intact. What compounds the nuisance is that this intellectual transaction will take us far from a discussion of form, out very far out, into some unexplored unfeasible regions. We will be talking after all about death, a subject intolerable to most, and are going to be taking the most witch-ridden aspect of it, for we will assume that death is not conventional death – death as the common end – but to the contrary, will talk of death as a continuation, a migration, a metamorphosis. That means we must now enter into speculation of an outrageous sort. And yet we must speculate, and in just such fashion, for if death is continuation – at least for some – then hints and portents are everywhere about us.

INTERVIEWER

So you now forsake all talk of form?

MAILER

I cannot explain form without talking of time. We are agreed upon that. But I think we should not talk about time unless we speculate about death.

INTERVIEWER

You've left me. Here you've left me.

MAILER

Death and time meet in critical fashion.

INTERVIEWER

Beware of banality.

MAILER

No, I am trying to say, and I don't know how to make it easy for you, that time is the continuation from life into death – it commands, if you will, both terminals of the tunnel – that is my supposition.

INTERVIEWER

It is a large one.

MAILER

I offer you something bigger. Soul and Time (if we may, for an instant, speak in the upper case) bear so profound a relation to one another, they are identical.

INTERVIEWER

The soul is equal to time?

MAILER

Nothing less.

INTERVIEWER

So you speak of the soul to explain form. You are neat today.

MAILER

Form, you said, is a shape in time. I try to suggest that the only measure of time – no, put it more directly – its only *container* is an enlifement, that mode or character or style by which time is perceived in each different kind of being. It is a way of saying that time does not have a universal existence, an overall existence like a blanket, nor is it even like a projectile carrying the universe in a cannonball; no, rather it is a set of separate creations similar to the points of pigment so close to light in the paintings of Seurat. Any general sense of time is then a fiction. A clock is a philosophical fiction among men, at best an accommodation between a hundred million or a million million separate creations, each embodying some separate continuation of (not a sense of time, but) time itself.

INTERVIEWER

Man is time?

MAILER

The soul of man is one kind of time.

INTERVIEWER

We are up the garden path by now.

MAILER

It is as far as I can go in this direction without devoting the next ten years to a study of physics, and physicists I have been assured get no new ideas after twenty. So let us slide over in our discussion from time to the more comfortable terrain of soul and death. Do you see already how more intimate they are?

INTERVIEWER

Classmates.

. . .

INTERVIEWER
I recapitulate. It seems to me you suggest that an appreciation of form is related to a comprehension of death, not my idea of death – that final sound I hear echoing in old stone walls and over the wind of burial grounds – but, no, your more athletic presentation of the matter, death as sea change, voyages, metamorphoses. So we have to talk of the soul, that damn *ghost*, and I don't know bean-pie of what you have in mind. I suspect you will carry me into some sort of discussion clear on the other side of the divide.

MAILER
What is your sense of what I have tried to say?

INTERVIEWER
I recollect that you were sufficiently carried away to speak yesterday of souls in food. Among other items, we fixed on a tin of sardines and spoke of the fortified soul of a superior sardine in the tin. I feel a little claustrophobic about that.

MAILER
I didn't extend the meaning of the word 'soul' beyond its own elasticity, I hope.

INTERVIEWER
Beyond any reasonable comprehension of its meaning? I think you did. Look! Once a body is dead – what do you do then with the soul? Do you contemplate it? Do you eat it? Once you get specific, you're drowning in sardine oil.

MAILER
Take the soul in that sardine. Can we proceed to eat it literally, and go on to think of it philosophically as the same entity which was once in the sardine's body?

INTERVIEWER

That is my question.

MAILER

Yes, can we eat that precise soul-and-body equal to one sardine which we chose yesterday to call one being? I don't know if we can. The intellectual discomfort is too great.

INTERVIEWER

You agree?

MAILER

It is too hard to imagine a soul in a body and alive; then alive without a body, yet unchanged – no, I think we can conceive of it remaining the same only in the way a light beam remains in some manner constant after it has been banked off a mirror, reflected through a lens, and bent in water. Such a light beam is now going in another direction, and for all we know is altered seriously in character; it may possess, for example, electromagnetic properties which are different from its previous possessions, just so different as its new direction. Still, we can say we are probably studying the same light beam we were looking at before its physical adventures. Let us try then to follow the transition, let us speculate upon it. When the soul inhabits a body, it tries to exercise its intent within that body. Sometimes it satisfies itself, often it fails, but it carries some instinct which leads it toward something mysterious, something I will be so mistaken as to now call the Vision (of which more later may be said) but since the word is capitalized let me say that I do not want to beg the quality of its character, nor imply it is routinely religious. The Vision may be beatific, heroic, epic, contemplative, tragic, harmonious, or even Faustian; the Vision may shift in its direction; perhaps it is capable of a Satanic contract – we do not know – each of us would indeed postulate a different kind of Vision. For now, it is enough to say that by our definition the soul has an instinct which leads it toward that part of the Vision it can sense or comprehend, and the soul – goes our next hypothesis – is resisted in this attempt by all those forces in the world, whose desire is to frustrate every soul in this attempt.

INTERVIEWER

You speak again of the Devil?

MAILER

For the moment I wish to emphasize only this: the body to which the soul is wed, or bound in love with, or at war against – forgive these legalisms, but that marriage here called soul-to-body is complex beyond imagination – yes, that body at any rate which is ground for a soul, sooner or later dies, it ceases to function, it enters a state of decomposition. Let us consider that.

INTERVIEWER

What then happens to the soul?

MAILER

Well, I would postulate a new condition for it. So long as it was part of a body, it was free, free existentially, it could attempt to do what it wished to do, it could war against everything which resisted it; if it failed, there was failure, but the attempt was at least possible. The soul existed as a dynamic will. And the reasons: it was part of a body which was able to change its environment. Yet once the body is dead, a soul is no longer free, or at least it is no longer free to alter its environment actively through the agency of a body. The body was its instrument; without such a tool, the soul enters a radically different state, for now it is passive and acted upon by environment.

INTERVIEWER

It is worn down, it is eroded. Like a material? Like a piece of driftwood?

MAILER

Yes.

INTERVIEWER

Can it be worn literally out of existence?

MAILER

I think it can be said that, other things being equal, it is worn down.

INTERVIEWER

But are you speaking of the soul as here having still a physical existence? It must if it is being worn down.

MAILER

It is idle how I speak of it. The soul may have some physical existence after the death of the body, or it may not—

INTERVIEWER

I'm sure everyone must talk in private like this.

MAILER

Jokes on your philosopher's vocabulary could be endless.

INTERVIEWER

Proceed. I will bridle my wit until it bleeds at the gums.

MAILER

Blood is the whisky of the soul. The point I try to make is that the soul, whether physical or immaterial, is still a creature of properties and desires, forced into the anguish of a situation largely more passive than before, so that whatever in its new situation is not essential to it must be lost. Unfree of an opportunity to act, it is acted upon by all the forces of man, nature, good will, ill will and the wind, and is therefore (in an absence of dramatic events) reduced down to a state where it can be reduced no more. At that point it is the essence of itself.

INTERVIEWER

You are speaking perhaps of the Greek conception of the atom, of that particle which cannot be divided further.

MAILER

That suggests a materiality we do not have to consider here. Even disembodied, the soul may still have a physical existence, or again it may not – we won't be so fancy as to say. But whether it is material, astral, spectral, or most modestly psychic, one likelihood presents itself – that it must take up an abode in some already prepared form which is independent of itself.

INTERVIEWER

So that is when it becomes attached to a body again?

MAILER

Oh, no. No, no. When a soul is an essential part of a being, it is born with the body and grows with the body, perhaps it is even present at the conception of the body. But I talk here rather of the soul in its outlaw state, after the death of the body. The new form it appropriates serves as a shell – we may almost view directly the hermit crab and the empty shell of the snail. The new form is a house, you see, not a body; unlike a body it is not capable of adapting to the demands or desires of the soul, and therefore the soul, an outlaw from life, has taken to it only from a kind of desperation, for we are assuming the most existential of conditions for this disembodied state, we are picturing the soul in a time of voyages, and anguish, and loss, the diminution of its properties. For protection it chooses an abode.

INTERVIEWER

You postulate this state as true for everyone who dies.

MAILER

I don't begin to postulate. I offer you images, that is all.

INTERVIEWER

Your presentation is perhaps too general to speak of images.

MAILER

Very well. Let us be precise. Think of the driftings of one particular soul; let it be the disembodiment of a man drowned at sea. This outlaw soul—

INTERVIEWER

You mean, this nautical soul.

MAILER

Call it a Salt. This Salt – disembodied – moves mutely through the water from object to object, from a mussel shell to a barnacle to a drift of seaweed torn from its embedment on the rocks. Finally it chooses a piece of wood whose shape is halfway agreeable to it, a piece of wood whose form is not unlike a particular human face which was once part of the memory of that soul. Of course, there may be other souls attached to the wood already; perhaps a battle of subtle influences is about to ensue; but this is certainly too novel-istic a situation to follow further at this point. Let us stay most impoverished. Let us stay lean and philosophical. Assume rather the wood is uninhabited except for our one particular soul which – notice this and bless it – proceeds by the salt of its conviction, by the crystallization of its pre-vious experience, to mobilize its conception of a face into that wood, and so etches the driftwood closer to the Salt's idea of a face it can use. Hold still on this and I'll try to explain what I mean by 'use'. A week goes by, a month; the wood is illumined by the Salt, which is to say it is *carved* by the soul, for the wood now is able to defend itself against the washing of the water, that is, it is worn down unequally with what is now a particular determination to save a few special artful parts of its potential form. Thrown up on shore, half the size it was, the wood is now more like the face the soul had glimpsed. Treated by the sun, it rots with dry design. One of us goes strolling along the beach, falls upon it, brings the driftwood back, brushes it, takes it home, and stares at the find. The face, created in part by the soul of the dead sailor, haunts us a little, it shapes our motives, just a touch – that Salt has entered us, just a touch, psychically.

INTERVIEWER

Not physically?

MAILER

That is yet to come. That is another epic.

INTERVIEWER

Sketch it.

MAILER

We change. We tire of the face, we put the driftwood into the fire and burn it. A whiff of smoke comes into our nostrils, shocking, clear, aromatic. It has character in its odor. Surprised, we breathe deep, and the Salt has entered our lungs, is now attached to a cell in the blood, red as a root. From that blood cell it must make its way through a thousand adventures to the sperm. It must travel through the perils of enzymes, catalysts, glands and juices, attach itself to and disconnect itself from molecule after molecule until it reaches a form which offers life.

INTERVIEWER

Like the protein molecule DNA, for example, in the chromosomes of a sperm?

MAILER

Something like that. Never doubt it.

INTERVIEWER

If this is religion, it is not agreeable. What is there of eternal slumber, universal verities? This is hectic.

MAILER

Call it ceaseless suffering.

INTERVIEWER

It is not rest.

MAILER

Still, it is an existence. The Salt clinging to a piece of wood can have the pleasure of drifting on an ocean of long summer swells, it can be warmed by the sun, lit by the moon, and even feel a fraction divine as it works along, rapt in the labor of working a design upon the wood. That Salt could say: I, now, subtly, inevitably, insinuate myself into form, I reveal the shape of my Being – just like God.

INTERVIEWER

But why? Why just like God – if indeed He is there – why would God wish to reveal the shape of *His* Being?

MAILER

It is the most elegant way He can communicate Himself, for it avoids the danger of communicating Himself to those who hate Him most.

INTERVIEWER

Do I follow? Not much.

MAILER

The pious response would be: the devil hates nature. I expect I must agree. Now, *I* am solemn. But it is reasonable to assume that the devil hates nature so much he cannot bear to look at it. He must name what he sees before he sees it. Or instantly after. He must dominate nature because it does not belong to him. That is why he cannot bear to contemplate it. (*Pause*)

INTERVIEWER

But now you are suddenly silent and don't go on.

MAILER

I am afraid. This inquiry we are pursuing satisfies a definition just given of the Satanic.

INTERVIEWER

I assure you, you are far from communicating yourself to this believer.

MAILER

(*Cheerfully*) Then perhaps it is safe to proceed.

INTERVIEWER

Nonetheless, you now look worried again. In fact, you look damn worried. It's just come all over you.

MAILER

I've been feeling a contradiction in everything I said earlier. There's something makes me uneasy. I am worrying the possibility that a soul must have something in kind to work upon, something in the driftwood which I might be forced to call spirit, the spirit of the driftwood. But this proposes an indigestible complication, and the truth is that I am a little uneasy of your temper. (*Holds up both hands to emphasize the measure*) Yes, I think we now say goodbye to all hope of arriving at anything elegant in our speculations. For at this instant, a hundred difficulties rush into the argument, and the first is the worst. I've just come to the grim conclusion that I must change the terms of our discussion, or to be less polite to myself, must now admit that I have to shift my terms around to include another mysterious element in these metamorphoses, an element I expect is far more mysterious than soul: spirit, yes spirit, spirit.

INTERVIEWER

What then! – you shift the terms – well, what then is spirit?

MAILER

That is what I am not sure of.

INTERVIEWER

Yet you choose to begin?

MAILER

I may become more certain as I talk. Often I do.

INTERVIEWER

Or contradict yourself further.

MAILER

Either.

INTERVIEWER

You are certainly an existentialist.

MAILER

I began to feel in trouble about the time we started to talk of the soul of the amoeba. Perhaps it does have one, but then, if you remember, I wasn't certain, I began to postulate the possibility that all the amoebae in the pond composed one exceptional soul. And that notion was unsatisfactory. I think what I was trying to say was that the soul of the pond was not a soul but a spirit. And now the idea becomes more clear because one can think more easily of some pullulating unhappy swarm of amoebae all making up the spirit of a slime on the pond, perhaps even a malignant and powerful slime which may be why you dislike amoebae so, and why, secretly, all the while I was promoting their virtues, I found them near to repulsive.

INTERVIEWER

That slime of amoebae on the pond – it is a spirit, you claim now? It is one kind of spirit?

MAILER

Yes.

INTERVIEWER

Tell me of others.

MAILER

I think it would be easier if you ask a few questions.

INTERVIEWER

Is the tree also a spirit?

MAILER

I have no idea. Maybe it is soul *and* spirit.

INTERVIEWER

Once again you've succeeded in whipping up our collective confusions.

MAILER

I feel new ideas emerging, but they make me uneasy. I remember I began to feel uneasy when I spoke of the amoeba as an army. An army after all is spirit.

INTERVIEWER

An army is made up of men. Of a hundred thousand men, we may say. Which by your count is one hundred thousand souls. Do all of these souls – one hundred thousand – make one spirit?

MAILER

So far as they give themselves to an effort thrust on them by some larger spirit *or* soul, why yes, then that part of them which is obedient to the army obviously contributes to the *function* of the army. (*Happily*) The function is the center of the spirit. That may be a beginning. Suppose that souls possess a personal life and thus are unpredictable and full of turns, but a spirit is a function. It can only wax strong or weak.

INTERVIEWER

Realize what you've said. You are implicating us in the idea that the cells in our body are spirits and souls. But cells certainly seem to possess far more of one or another specific function than any suggestion of a personal life. They must be spirits.

MAILER

Perhaps they are.

INTERVIEWER

Then you do overthrow much of what you said earlier. And I have no idea of what bearing this has on form.

MAILER

My difficulty is that I do not necessarily have a message to unfold which was once carefully folded. Rather my problem may vary from severing a series of knots to excavating a tomb.

INTERVIEWER

There are too many ideas at once.

MAILER

Yes. Could it be that a cell is a spirit composed of many souls?

INTERVIEWER

A parenthesis: (From where do these souls arrive?)

MAILER

(From their travels.)

INTERVIEWER

And where in the cell are they to be found?

MAILER

In the nucleus if it will make you happy. In the chromosomes of the nucleus. In your DNA molecule. In particles too small for the electron microscope to discover. God knows. Their precise residence is not a part of this discussion.

INTERVIEWER

But the spirit of the cell rules over the souls within that cell. It makes them offer up allegiance to the government of the spirit?

MAILER

Yes. I will say yes.

INTERVIEWER

A man – a soul! – would, however, command the spirits of his cells?

MAILER

More or less. If he is in command of his cells. If a malignancy had not begun. But forgive me for these examples. They lead but to further confusion.

INTERVIEWER

Still, if one is to stake out the ground in a general way – anything to keep your metaphor afloat – I could go on to ask if people considered in social groups may be seen as collections of *whole souls* – engrave those words! – or if such associations are not too loose to be termed spirits.

MAILER

Some spirits are cohesive, some are not. A bag of beans is probably a spirit – a very weak one, of course.

INTERVIEWER

Groups of men form spirits then, some loose, some cohesive. Yes? In turn the collision of these spirits makes a nation?

MAILER

Yes.

INTERVIEWER

A nation which has a soul? A soul over all these spirits?

MAILER

Some nations seem to have a soul.

INTERVIEWER

Some seem to have a spirit. Soul. Spirit. You have opened a pair of categories which are hopeless. Some people have spirits, others have soul?

MAILER

Yes.

INTERVIEWER

Characterize the difference. Make at least some attempt. What is the difference to me if I am a soul or a spirit?

MAILER

A creature who is a spirit is hardly the same as a man who has spirit. Someone who has spirit is a soul, a fortunate soul, rather a powerful soul.

INTERVIEWER

Whereas, someone who *is* a spirit is selfless?

MAILER

Precisely. The sort of people we say are full of soul actually are spirits. Beautiful spirits perhaps.

INTERVIEWER

That helps a bit. Still you spoke earlier of a cell which might have a soul *and* a spirit. There is a ladder of dominations you seem to be always about to construct – spirit dominated by a soul who in turn is dominated by a higher spirit which is then dominated by yet a higher soul. Just as we are about to arrive, you confound the two together again. If we are to avoid intolerable ambiguities, you must now try to speak in some decent detail about the properties of soul and spirit, the more particular properties. You must try to separate them.

MAILER

Suppose I define soul by saying it is a sort of creature, doubtless invisible, which has a purchase on eternity. It also has an individual life, a *personal* life, which is contained in itself, and this personal life is carried through its metamorphoses. It is the soul's character in the same way the taste of the sardine is the sardine's character.

INTERVIEWER

Is this character immutable?

MAILER

Of course not. It can change as quickly as a taste can rot. But it is at least continuous. Change in character is the continuing line of the soul.

INTERVIEWER

You speak of character. Is this the moral character of the soul?

MAILER

The Vision is moral. The soul, as we suggested, works its way toward the Vision. But the soul is itself amoral.

INTERVIEWER

Oh, no! Just when I was beginning to understand.

MAILER

I've been too timid in this exposition. We are not dealing with logic but metaphor. Metaphor exists to contain contradiction. I repeat: the soul is amoral. Its purpose is not to be ethical, but to live. Its desire is to live. So long as it is a healthy soul, its nourishment comes from growth and victory, from exploration, from conquest, from pomp and pageant and triumph, from glory. Is this sufficiently simple for you? It lives for stimulation, for pleasure. It abhors defeat. Its nature is to become more than it is.

INTERVIEWER

But you might just as well be talking of a Roman. Worse. The soul according to you has no impulse to civilize a thing.

MAILER

Civilization is a spirit. I propose to you that the soul is an animal carrying a burden of existence toward the Vision. Like an animal the soul is able to fight, to endure, to war, to kill, to flee, to become lean, wily, hard, a mink, a minx, a wild cat, puma, leopard or tiger. The soul can even descend within a body, and assume the secret sluggish wisdom of a clam, resist change with the force of a clam's valve.

INTERVIEWER

What sort of person would have a soul like a clam?

MAILER

A banker. A banker of the worst sort.

INTERVIEWER

A fair image. Can the soul have no gentle qualities?

MAILER

It can become brave like a lion, noble like a good ape, it can grow as distrustful as an owl, as graceful as a cat, or fierce as a lobster.

INTERVIEWER

Can it love? Can the soul feel love?

MAILER

(*Carried away*) Like a frump, like a poodle, like a fury. Passion comes from the soul. But the soul can only love what offers it growth. It loves most what offers it the happiest, richest growth. It detests sickness, dying, death.

INTERVIEWER

Yet by your definition Romeo and Juliet loved with their soul.

MAILER

Yes. And died for it.

INTERVIEWER

Exactly. They died for love. I thought the soul detested death?

MAILER

It does. The only true and passionate lovers are those who love each other because they give life to one another.

INTERVIEWER

What kind of life?

MAILER

Whatever the particular soul needs most. If it needs violence, it will love the violent. There are souls which can be expressed – that is, *un*deadened – only by violence.

INTERVIEWER

You make the soul sound like the unconscious.

MAILER

But of course it is the unconscious. What did you think it was?

INTERVIEWER

Very well, then. Can the soul be drawn to compassion, to justice, to order?

MAILER

To the degree that an animal can. Perhaps a little more.

INTERVIEWER

An animal has need of justice?

MAILER

An animal dies from injustice. The soul needs justice much as it needs air. But few souls can offer justice.

INTERVIEWER

Compassion?

MAILER

I expect it is even more rare than justice. Still the soul cannot do without the giving of compassion and the receiving of it.

INTERVIEWER

Doesn't the offering of compassion sometimes interfere with one's own growth? Since one must give rather than receive, so the soul is obliged to dispense a part of its wealth?

MAILER

In offering compassion, some souls feel an exquisite sense of beauty.

INTERVIEWER

The soul needs beauty?

MAILER

Like the body needs food.

INTERVIEWER

Why?

MAILER

Beauty is the blood and bone of the soul.

INTERVIEWER

I thought whisky was the blood of the soul.

MAILER

Let us say whisky is the blood and vinegar of the soul.

INTERVIEWER

All right. Now I have a picture. Of sorts. I still don't know why Romeo and Juliet died for love if the soul detests death, and I certainly don't know why if beauty is the blood and bone of the soul, you have so many fucking souls going around blasting up beauty and destroying it, but I think it would be better to wait. I do not want complications here.

MAILER

Oh, they are coming again.

INTERVIEWER

I'm convinced of it. Still I've got some grip at last on what you're talking about. For soul, at any rate. I understand it except for one thing. If it is eternal—

MAILER

Yes.

INTERVIEWER

—why then is it so active?

MAILER

One reason is the metamorphosis from one life to another.

INTERVIEWER

I know about that, I think. It is poor man's Yoga. The soul resides in a cow in one life, a squid in the next, a man – ugh, what a man coming from a cow and a squid – in the third, a cockroach in the fourth, a brave cockroach, to a tulip in the fifth, very self-complacent; it blooms into a blade of grass in the sixth.

MAILER

The migration sometimes turns out more modest.

INTERVIEWER

Rich Episcopalian, Presbyterian, modest Methodist,

Negro Baptist, Puerto Rican Catholic? This is very poor man's Yoga.

MAILER

I neglected to tell you that we are still far from Yoga. I think there is a Western obsession in the soul, a continuing obsession, which is at the source of its activity, its anxiety, its insomnia, its mania, its violence, its despair.

INTERVIEWER

Yes, now you're going to take me by surprise. I feel it. What are you about to claim as the continuing obsession of the soul?

MAILER

It wonders if it will continue to exist, or if it will perish.

INTERVIEWER

I thought you said the soul was eternal.

MAILER

It has a purchase on eternity. It can manage to live forever. But only if it *manages* to do so. Only if it is not finally defeated.

INTERVIEWER

So a soul can be eternal or die?

MAILER

Yes. It can die.

INTERVIEWER

That is the reason everything is so important to it? Is that why it feels such anxiety about its particular metamorphosis, or even the place where as an outlaw soul it may choose to take up its abode, whether in the mussel shell or the seaweed?

MAILER

Yes.

INTERVIEWER

That is why it is so fierce, and so animal when once in a body? That is why even if it needs beauty it might wish still to destroy it?

MAILER

Yes.

INTERVIEWER

Good. Something grows clear to me. In the suffering of the soul you talked about, in its anguish that it might be diminishing or coming close to a final death, there was a glimpse of another anguish. For many people there must be no other choice than to destroy something of beauty, or watch something of value die within themselves. So I wonder – would you agree to an elementary formula: if there is a God and a Devil both, and God creates beauty, then the Devil must attempt to steal it.

MAILER

Yes. And often he succeeds.

INTERVIEWER

How?

MAILER

By communicating himself to every pore of beauty. By convincing beauty it must fear whatever is good. And in fact, it must. Those who are good often hate beauty; they have been betrayed by it too many times. They know the devil which has come to live in beauty, that devil whose pleasure is to defeat possibility, deaden hope, waste effort. Therefore they feel as if they are killing the Devil when they loot the gallery. You see, in their mind, beauty is synonymous to waste.

INTERVIEWER

Do I keep up with you?

MAILER

Our soul needs beauty for its growth. But beauty is ready forever to betray it. So all too often the soul while remaining very much alive, nonetheless ceases to grow. It becomes timid. It is drawn to beauty, but beauty destroys its possibilities. A fearful tension is begun. It is in the soul's nature to grow, to seek growth. That is not only its pleasure but its duty. It knows – I'm afraid I quote myself – that if it does not grow, it must pay more for remaining the same. Yet each time beauty slays a possibility, some nerve is blunted. A death begins within which must finally be passed out, or the soul is stifled. So the soul turns to murder.

INTERVIEWER

Tragic.

MAILER

You bet. Left to itself the soul might always look for the kind of love which would offer the greatest possible growth. But, in life, nobody or almost nobody comes within a million human beings of whom he really needs. Spirits and shattered communications lie between the soul and a clear sense of its desire. Anyone who searches seriously for love comes to realize it is more difficult to find than the Holy Grail, or the way to Kafka's castle. So that is why Romeo and Juliet kill themselves, each separately, each by choice. They know they will not find such a love again in life. Therefore they are ready to search for one another across eternity. That offers more life to their soul than the bleak hope of recovery and new love. But for any situation which is not tragic, the soul detests death and abhors suicide.

INTERVIEWER

Why? Why not choose suicide often in order to hasten into the next stage?

MAILER

Because deep in the economy of Being, huge waste must be caused by any indiscriminate odyssey of souls, any incoherent metamorphoses.

INTERVIEWER

Eternity desires tidiness?

MAILER

Not as a passion, but as a use, as a most useful function.

INTERVIEWER

You make eternity sound like a neat old spinster.

MAILER

You think of eternity as some complacent cerulean vault which can afford tidiness or untidiness. But I use the word in the existential sense where eternity is not automatically eternal.

INTERVIEWER

Eternity means not eternal?

MAILER

Eternity means the will and the possibility to be eternal. Whether it can succeed is another matter. Eternity can perish. Tidiness and some reasonable law of order are as necessary therefore to its survival as lack of clutter on a sailing ship.

INTERVIEWER

We are outward bound?

MAILER

I do not feel we are coming home.

INTERVIEWER

Eternity is on a voyage?

MAILER

Life and eternity are on a voyage, yes.

INTERVIEWER

To go where?

MAILER

Out. Out to where whatever created us wishes us to be, out to where it was conceived we would move.

INTERVIEWER

And we have not gone as far as we were supposed to go?

MAILER

I think we have not gone near to far enough.

INTERVIEWER

All right. I can take a breath on that. (*Lights a cigarette*) I suppose I have to. I've got a picture of the soul. Yes, it's clear. But spirit. Oh, yes. I knew I had something to be depressed about. There's spirit. Even thinking about it, I know I'm nowhere near spirit – it feels like a wet paper bag over my head. Tell me, is a spirit as capable of dying as a soul?

MAILER

(*Long pause*) I would assume its existence is never alive, not finally alive in the way a soul is alive. In that sense spirit does not die, it cannot – it is never really alive. Rather it waxes strong or weak – like a function. But it does not die. It ebbs.

INTERVIEWER

But spirit is the medium, the solution if you will, into which soul submerges after each little death?

MAILER

It is the culture, the nutrient, it is the abode; not the body, but the abode; as the driftwood was an abode for the Salt.

INTERVIEWER

A soul passes then through spirit after it dies, after its little death, the one which makes it ready for its metamorphosis?

MAILER

I think it must. Perhaps it passes through many spirits.

INTERVIEWER

I'm going to be brutal. Forgive the lack of amenities, but spirit as I see it is a collection of souls without bodies, a collection station for what you call outlaw souls.

MAILER

Presumably the soul passes through spirit. It is not however sealed permanently in it. Not necessarily. It may merely be working for it. Often against its will. On the other hand, I think a spirit may contain any number of souls who have lost the power to find further metamorphoses, souls no longer eternal but rootless, alienated from existence, souls which can no longer grow within a body. So they pass permanently into spirit. They are the part of spirit which gives spirit a character, a discontent, a demonic fury. A hurricane might be such a spirit.

INTERVIEWER

Spirit is then some kind of psychic embodiment?

MAILER

I think it can be material as well. Spirit is not so clear an entity as soul. Spirit tends to *not* delineate its existence. Think of the cluster of one-celled animals in a Portuguese man-of-war. That is one kind of spirit. But the example is too clear. There are spirits you cannot picture. Psychic spirits. Like a habit.

INTERVIEWER

A habit is a spirit?

MAILER

A predictable spirit.

INTERVIEWER

What is a lively spirit?

MAILER

A gay little brook.

INTERVIEWER

All right, then. What is the largest spirit of which you can conceive?

MAILER

The heavens.

INTERVIEWER

I meant to ask for the largest spirit we might both be able to see.

MAILER

The ocean.

INTERVIEWER

Speak of a large spirit which has a shape.

MAILER

Of objects which have a shape, I would think of a mountain range or a cave.

INTERVIEWER

And what is the smallest spirit?

MAILER

A virus, I suspect.

INTERVIEWER

But the very smallest you could still see?

MAILER

A mildew or a mold. A drop of oil.

INTERVIEWER

What would be the most miserable spirit?

MAILER

A common cold.

INTERVIEWER

And the most palpable?

MAILER

A mood.

INTERVIEWER

What would be the most dramatic?

MAILER

A revolutionary spirit.

INTERVIEWER

And the most material?

MAILER

A tin of sardines.

INTERVIEWER

So now we have findings (of all sorts!) and may draw propositions, if we can find needles in haystacks. A soul, as I see it – this strapping little bugger – comes to the end of his existence in one body, and therefore enters a spirit for rest and necessary rehabilitation until the happy day he succeeds in moving his soul over to an embryo just begun.

MAILER

Yes.

INTERVIEWER

Then spirit must be always in flux. Souls coming in, souls saying farewell.

MAILER

You may think of a girls' dormitory.

INTERVIEWER

A spirit has no form?

MAILER

No form. It is a purpose, not an embodiment.

INTERVIEWER

What about the tin of sardines?

MAILER

The form of that is the form of the tin can. It could be filled with wax or honey or anchovies and look the same. Spirit is not apparent in the form but in the presence. You would have to open the can to discover the presence.

INTERVIEWER

Do I understand you? A mountain peak is a spirit, but it is also a form.

MAILER

It is a presence. One could cut a road through it, and the spirit would alter, but not because its shape was changed, but because birds left a hillside. It is a presence.

INTERVIEWER

You say a cold is a spirit, but it has a form. It has a shape in time, a run of symptoms.

MAILER

The symptoms do not make up a shape – rather they are

indications that something is shrinking out of time. A cold is a presence which speaks of a partial death of soul.

INTERVIEWER
A partial death of soul?

MAILER
A loss of some part of soul.

INTERVIEWER
Can soul be lost in part?

MAILER
As particularly as a limb can be amputated from a body. A soul can lose its best qualities, its courage, its compassion, its grace, or it can slough off its worst features, its cowardice, its terror, its avarice, its sloth. A soul is changed by inhabiting a body. At the time of its little death, it is better or it is worse than when it entered that body. Its form has altered.

INTERVIEWER
But when it enters a spirit it does not retain its form?

MAILER
At such a time, it has a potential form, but no body. It has a style, it has a character. Given the opportunity it will try to shape creation in its fashion. I refer you to the piece of driftwood.

INTERVIEWER
But, ultimately, the soul must find a body?

MAILER
It must be present in some way at a conception.

INTERVIEWER
Might it not have to wait for centuries?

MAILER

It would have to wait long, I would think. Unless it was an exceptional soul.

INTERVIEWER

And then?

MAILER

It might so illumine the spirit in which it found itself that the spirit would encourage an act of conception which the soul could join.

INTERVIEWER

For instance?

MAILER

A moonlit night on a lake. A swimmer drowns saving a child. His exceptional soul might then rise to the moon, be gilded when the moon is full, ride back on a beam and glide into a lover's act. He could be conceived in the first moment after he died.

INTERVIEWER

But what if the exceptional soul had the bad fortune to be trapped in a lesser spirit? The spirit of a common cold?

MAILER

Why he might relax the sufferer and stir their sex.

INTERVIEWER

But a more ordinary soul?

MAILER

Would have to wait a period in any spirit in which it found itself. There might be no occasion for a leap.

INTERVIEWER

The soul can find a new body only by a leap?

MAILER

One would think so.

INTERVIEWER

A literal or a metaphorical leap?

MAILER

Either.

INTERVIEWER

But if no leap suggests itself, one must wait. Isn't it grievous to wait in a spirit?

MAILER

I could not suggest.

INTERVIEWER

Do you know I still have no real sense of what a soul is – I think I know, and then I realize I can't quite distinguish it from a spirit, at least not when it is once in the soup.

MAILER

But we have not said nearly enough about spirit. There's the difficulty. I've just come to the conclusion a spirit must be led by a soul. By a soul which has lost eternity.

INTERVIEWER

I am fortified to hear that every spirit has a leader. Would you offer an example?

MAILER

Every house is a spirit. Except, perhaps, a new ranch house. So every house has a leader. A fine house might have a cricket under the stair. Of course the leader can just as easily be a poor creation, an owl, a termite, a cockroach, an earthworm in the cellar. There are corporation buildings with walls of glass and aisles of stainless steel whose leader is a bitter confirmed molecule of urine adhering to the drain in the executives' urinal.

INTERVIEWER

Such a leader cannot last very long.

MAILER

He could surprise you. Some molecules are crab-shaped and adhere to the porcelain for years. Of course all the urine going by does its best to dislodge it. But the moment such a leader succumbs he is replaced immediately by another molecule very much like himself.

INTERVIEWER

That is the spirit of the corporation?

MAILER

The spirit of the corporation extends over its buildings, factories, stocks, workers, commodities, salesmen, advertising agencies, and so on. I was speaking only of the main office.

INTERVIEWER

What of the spirit of the total corporation? Who is its leader?

MAILER

A mind without a body. A soul which died forever.

INTERVIEWER

Some major soul?

MAILER

A large soul but not a major soul. Not a dramatic soul – certainly not a dramatic soul.

INTERVIEWER

This is becoming agreeable, but I'm going to bring it up short. Because I don't think you realize that you're now saying a spirit can also be an organism.

MAILER

I think it is more like a field, or a mood. A presence. If it is an embodiment, a slice of meat for instance, it still has no body, not in the sense of a set of organs which function with one another.

INTERVIEWER

But a corporation has such organs.

MAILER

Yes, but the organs of a corporation are not materially connected.

INTERVIEWER

So a spirit can have shape or be shapeless, have organs or be bereft of them, can be seen or invisible, can have odor, color, taste, or no properties at all.

MAILER

Yes.

INTERVIEWER

Air? Is air a spirit?

MAILER

Air is filled with spirits and is itself a spirit.

INTERVIEWER

So spirits inhabit other spirits.

MAILER

Oh yes.

INTERVIEWER

And souls-in-bodies can inhabit spirits? Souls-in-bodies! I mean, people.

MAILER

Yes, people can be a part of many spirits. In a sense, all words are spirit.

INTERVIEWER

In precisely that sense, I shall soon become a part of the spirit of vertigo.

MAILER

Think of an ambitious advertising executive. He works for the main office of the corporation we just discussed. He is obedient to the spirit of the main office. To that molecule of urine. He goes to Mass on Sunday. He is a good Catholic. He belongs, he is a small part of the considerably more indefinable spirit of the Catholic Church. He is a sports fan. He roots for a major-league team, which is a sharply defined spirit, but since it is about to move to a new stadium in a different city, he will soon be less a part of its sharply defined spirit. At midnight he regularly watches a television host on a variety show.

INTERVIEWER

This television host is the leader of a spirit?

MAILER

He is the leader of a television audience. It is a wide spirit but not an incisive one.

INTERVIEWER

Then a spirit is a convocation?

MAILER

As we said earlier, yes.

INTERVIEWER

An assemblage?

MAILER

Yes.

INTERVIEWER

A collection?

MAILER

Yes, it is any of these.

INTERVIEWER

And yet, to return to this point, to return again to a point which is too simple or too mysterious for me, I wonder how a cell can be a spirit. It is an organism, not a convocation.

MAILER

But a cell is not free. The average cell is part of a larger organism.

INTERVIEWER

Let us say it is a part of the liver. The liver is an organ. Does the liver have a soul?

INTERVIEWER

It may or it may not. In most cases I expect it does.

INTERVIEWER

But the liver is not free of the body.

MAILER

It can have freedom within the body. It can choose to cooperate with the body, or merely to put up with the body. It can do its best to cure itself when it is ill, or it can fold up on itself like an invalid, and call to other portions of the body for aid.

INTERVIEWER

You speak of organs as if they were states or countries.

MAILER

They have character, like nations. They too can be spirits or souls. Or close to nothing at all.

INTERVIEWER

And it is freedom, the very limited freedom of the liver which allows it to be a soul?'

MAILER

France may be free, but it is not free to detach itself from the earth and ascend to the moon. It is not unnatural to speak of the soul of an organ. It is merely a soul with a fixed position. Its freedom lies elsewhere.

INTERVIEWER

But there are organs which are spirits, you say.

MAILER

Yes, finally I will agree. There are organs which are spirits and organisms which are spirits. They are without freedom. They are obedient to an external will. By themselves they are not able to adapt to new conditions. So there is a limit to how much they can help the body.

INTERVIEWER

A while ago you seemed to indicate that a spirit was not alive, not alive as an organism. You spoke of houses, systems of plumbing, of air, hurricanes, common colds, the ocean. Now you speak of organisms and organs and call them spirits.

MAILER

Spirits are habits, not innovations; functions, not creations; waves, not forms; not so much the act as the context; never the event, but the institution. So there are even people whom one may call spirits. Some years ago there was a fashion to call them other-directed.

INTERVIEWER

By now, have you not violated every category altogether?

MAILER

Not if we hold to the primary distinction. A spirit, no matter how close it approaches resemblance to a soul, is still a being in which something vital has died.

INTERVIEWER

But how would you define what is vital?

MAILER

It is a grasp upon the present which enables you to alter it in surprising fashion.

INTERVIEWER

Is this another way of saying that a human being becomes a spirit if his soul has died?

MAILER

If the soul has died while right within the body, if it has died finally right there, has ceased to exist forever, ceased to exist in eternity, then the living body remaining in such a man has become a spirit.

INTERVIEWER

Such a man could not create life?

MAILER

He could create life, but still be a spirit.

INTERVIEWER

How is that? Don't you betray your last distinction?

MAILER

The soul may exist still within the body, but it has surrendered.

INTERVIEWER

Surrendered what?

MAILER

Its hope of eternity.

INTERVIEWER

How fearful a state that must be.

MAILER

I think we all have intimations of such a condition.

INTERVIEWER

Still – it must be very painful. Yet, you are not logically scrupulous, you pass by a distinction which is most crucial. I ask you: if a man can create children, how can you say that he has nonetheless surrendered his hope of eternity?

MAILER

His children could be somebody else's purchase on eternity. Perhaps our sperm does not contain our soul, but others with their own separate chain of metamorphoses. Remember the effort of the Salt to return to the blood and the root? It could have been a stranger's blood, a stranger's root.

INTERVIEWER

Too poetic. And too quick. You deprive us of the claim that there are families in which a soul may reappear in a man's descendants. Don't forget you spoke earlier about the tidiness of eternity.

MAILER

Yes, I am not here to say it is impossible. Probably we are talking of the unspoken impulse behind family vaults and plots.

INTERVIEWER

Yes, if eternity is well managed, that would account for the weakness some of my friends feel before titles, or speaking to families of unbroken line.

MAILER

Yes, that could explain their weakness.

INTERVIEWER

Think of the metamorphoses in such a family. Why, they could move in a direct line. The body, just expired, of the master of the house is taken from the master bedroom to the family crypt. Presto! He is back from the tomb and bawling in the nursery, an infant now forced to put up with all the ice of a British infancy. It is orderly. It accounts for the complacency, the solidity, and the strength of certain families. They know the Lord does not have to put Himself out for them, and bear with migrations which travel too far and exhaust too much of His time.

MAILER

Once this used to be true, I'm sure.

INTERVIEWER

You think death now refuses to be so accommodating?

MAILER

Perhaps. It is restless. Modern death gives a hint of horror – as if it goes in two directions at once. Sometimes I think God may have lost His way.

INTERVIEWER

How could He have lost His way?

MAILER

He could be too far behind. We could have been too slow. Too many of us might have died, too many surrendered. God no longer knows whether to reduce our migrations to the family plot, or encourage the most exceptional surrealist journey.

INTERVIEWER

Brilliant! If you are saying that surrealism speaks of the migration of souls.

MAILER

It speaks of metamorphoses. Frightening metamorphoses. Startling metamorphoses. Teacups come to look like heads, and bodies turn to wooden toys. I am saying that eternity does not offer the rest it once possessed.

INTERVIEWER

You are so unhappy about all this. You insist that death is now worse than it has been.

MAILER

It is restless. The thought of death is equal to dread for the modern soul. Talk of the possibilities within death gives cheer to no one any longer. Maybe we are told each night in our sleep (by the great spirit of sleep!) that death is not the end of anything, but is instead a continuation of the worst terrors of life. Perhaps that is why people wish to see death as the end, as a final conclusion. It may be too awful to contemplate the debt there is to be paid each time the body dies (whatever that debt may be) and how do you bear your anguish if the soul must sink to a lower existence? There is always the terror that you may finally betray the deepest value of your experience. Besides, the soul must bear the weight of continuing to exist. Much of existence is now war; it is a grim war for most.

INTERVIEWER

A war against whom? Against what?

MAILER

Against the desire of something, some spirit perhaps, that life should end.

INTERVIEWER

Life end? Why should it? Why should there be a spirit which wishes life to cease?

MAILER

Life may now be intolerable to some other conception of Being – I would not know what else to call it but a plague – which is different from ourselves, more powerful perhaps, some conception so antagonistic to the Vision by which we try to discover our life that its presence has invaded our world, perhaps even our universe. The intent of such a plague is to deaden the soul of all of us, invite it to surrender.

INTERVIEWER

Couldn't the Devil be this spirit?

MAILER

Perhaps he is. But who can know? Perhaps the plague wishes to destroy spirit. Perhaps the plague collaborates with spirit.

INTERVIEWER

Is this plague equal to the Devil?

MAILER

Again I have no idea. Perhaps it wishes to destroy the Devil along with everything else. Perhaps the Devil bears the same relation to the plague that Faust bears to Mephisto.

INTERVIEWER

But whichever it is, the plague wishes that life cease to exist?

MAILER

Yes.

INTERVIEWER

And time would then cease?

MAILER

Time by our scheme is Being in its becoming, so time would cease.

INTERVIEWER

This bears, I suppose, some relation to Nietzsche's dictum that God is dead.

MAILER

Other than a suggestion that God is mortal, it bears no relation.

INTERVIEWER

Well, that saves time. In fact, you believe that God can be either eternal, or perish?

MAILER

His nature is to be eternal if He succeeds in remaining eternal. If He is not destroyed.

INTERVIEWER

Yes. I follow that. When you speak of the surrender of souls, it is as if you make the totality of them synonymous to God.

MAILER

They are not synonymous. There is the Spirit and the Vision as well. You must account for the Spirit and the Vision.

INTERVIEWER

But souls are the essence of God? His *élan vital*? His flux?

MAILER

They are His present tense. His moral nature exists, you remember, not in the soul but in the Vision. Good I will give you a scheme. It will make you happy. Vision is the mind of God; soul, His body; and Spirit is what He has left behind. Literally. It is His excrement.

INTERVIEWER

So bad as that?

MAILER

Not so bad. Moral nature resides after all in the Spirit as well as the Vision.

INTERVIEWER

In the Spirit? In God's excrement? In the Devil?

MAILER

Think of this Devil as the echo of history, the lore of the past, the mansions of philosophy, as the blunt weight of every problem which has been solved and every lie which has succeeded. Think of this Devil as the spirit of magic and the dead spirit of institutional life, as mass communication, and the passing of the guards. Everything rich, hideous, poor, proud, nauseating and marvelous goes into that excrement, but it is God's excrement – it is more so. So take Spirit and pose it upon the Vision of the future – between just these two leviathans, at their junction, is moral nature. Of course this moral nature, this junction, is being rotted by the plague.

INTERVIEWER

You balance a cliché like a barbell. What I do not comprehend is whether this new Spirit with its capital S, this new property of God, is the same vast malign spirit which seeks to obliterate Time, or if it is some other Spirit altogether, a visitor from out of somewhere. Or has the Spirit of God become diseased by the plague? I see you preparing to object – you are about to say that you cannot possibly know the answer, your admission that you do not know where to place the Devil in relation to plague is the answer, that my question is therefore insulting because repetitious, yet I would present to you that the essential presumption of the enterprise makes one almost disappointed you are not ready to answer. For consider: what you have stated up to here is so obviously a philosophy of hugely paranoid proportions that for your own sake and for a general inspiring of confidence one would hope you are ready to offer some hint of a few objective criteria, some warrant that your ideas are not merely a projection from the eye of your brain to the wall of your brain. Now, I know it's getting late, and this is a demand of proportions – I can see by your eye that you think it's getting very late—

MAILER

Objective criteria overwhelm us. Their signs are everywhere.

INTERVIEWER

You will tell me the invasion of this malign spirit presents itself in flying saucers?

MAILER

Of course not. No need for saucers. Though nothing has to cause surprise, for existence approaches a climax.

INTERVIEWER

What then are the objective criteria? Display them.

MAILER

They show themselves in every crack of every detail in our lives, in the processing of our food is one seat of the plague, and in the plastic commodities we handle, the odor of vaginal jelly, the dead character of public communication, the pollution of air, the collective assaults upon human nerve.

INTERVIEWER

Are these criteria? or merely temporary technological trials? – just a list of your familiar prejudices?

MAILER

Look to the forms. The forms of the modern world break down. That is where you find all objective criteria – in the art of the twentieth century, above all in the architecture, in the empty monotonous interchangeable statements of our modern buildings.

INTERVIEWER

Not that again! Not all this reduced to still one more of your endless diatribes about modern architecture.

MAILER

I'm talking not of architecture but of form. Form is the deepest clue we possess to the nature of time in any epoch, to the style of the time, to the mode by which reality is perceived in the time, to the way time moves in the consciousness of man, where it possesses grace, where it is hobbled, how strength addresses itself to weakness. Time is all but equal to creativity, for time is the potential to create as it resides in each of us. So form is the clue to the vitality or lethargy of time, and the most pervasive forms of the modern world speak now of an absence of invention, a pall upon good spirit, an erosion of memory. Only in the corners is there preoccupation with complexity of form, with these interruptions of time we comprehend in the absurd. Full of feverish creativity and feverish destruction are the forms in the corners and the edges – in the center is nothing but an aesthetic desert, those pillars of salt which rise out of the plains of urban renewal, out of the triumph of that totalitarian spirit whose impulse is to betray form, to abstract form, until the meanings in its creation are lost. The passion of totalitarianism is to conceal its own process; so its passion is to abstract form into monotony for monotonous forms are superior at concealing the sinister processes of their creation since it drains vitality to study them. That bleakness of form speaks of an apathy in the heart of time, and by implication – a terror, an exhaustion. No rest. (*Sways slightly*)

INTERVIEWER

Not, I fear, in this metamorphosis. (*Smiles*) Tell me, when did eternity possess the sort of rest of which you speak?

MAILER

Why, when the Greeks thrived, the Goths hunted, and the Renaissance came to Rome, the guillotine to France.

INTERVIEWER

You look fatigued. I will not ask you more. Do you wish to end here?

MAILER

Not at all. But *you* look in need of a drink. So I take pity on us both, and crack out a glass.

INTERVIEWER

We have not finished properly.

MAILER

No. We have not even begun to discuss the subject. There is so much of which to talk. I have not mentioned the positive properties of spirit, the fields of communication it lays open, that subtle intimate collaboration of soul and spirit in everything alive, the secrets of grace where soul and spirit commune. (*Bitterly*) No, as always, I have spent my time talking of disease. But then, there is no end to metaphysics, they say. (*Stands up*) This is the place we stop, I offer you one last question. You may ask anything.

INTERVIEWER

Soon they will be reading your book. This book. This is therefore the moment for us to end and book reviewers to begin So I would ask you — what is form?

MAILER

Did I not explain?

INTERVIEWER

You certainly didn't.

MAILER

My God!

INTERVIEWER

Is it now too late?

MAILER

My God. I could have sworn I explained it a thousand times.

INTERVIEWER

You did, but then you didn't. You see, now I know that form, and shape, and space, and time, and even death, I suppose, each give off their own special taste to every little pickle in the pickle barrel, but no, I could not tell a soul in five easy words just what we mean by form.

MAILER

I must help you. Certainly I must. Here, have a drink. (*Passes ice and glasses*) Maybe we must go back to the drift-wood again. (*Scratches his head*) Is that too long a way for you to go back?

INTERVIEWER

Now that I have a drink it is easy.

MAILER

Driftwood is a fine form. It expresses the essence of form.

INTERVIEWER

Why? Why the essence!

MAILER

Because it proclaims the value of what is kept. Form always makes one tacit statement – it says: I am a definite *form* of existence, I choose to have character and quality, I choose to be recognizable, I am – everything considered – the best that could be done under the circumstances, and so superior to a blob.

INTERVIEWER

Bravo!

MAILER

Yes, driftwood is a fine form. It tells us what in a piece of wood proved most dear to the wood, what resisted decomposition the longest, what – if we know how to read it – was saved by accident, what was etched by design. The form of driftwood is the record of a siege.

INTERVIEWER

But driftwood rots from the outside in – which suggests that its center is not so much essential as most protected?

MAILER

What is most valuable is usually most protected. When the center is not valuable, it rots, it rots first. Occasionally we see driftwood which has hollows in its heart or holes. Form in general – now I let you in on the secret – is the record of a war.

INTERVIEWER

Of a war? Damn you! Of a war?

MAILER

It is the record, as seen in a moment of rest; yes, it is the record of a war which has been taking place. Don't you see whatever is alive, or intent, or obsessed, must wage an active war: it creates the possibility for form in its environment by its every attempt to shape the environment. Wherever the environment resists, the result is a form. When the soul is mighty and the environment resists mightily, the form is exceptional or extraordinary. Sometimes it speaks of what is great or exquisite. Stone hoisted up ramps by men became the pyramids. Cut by crude iron tools and harder stone, shaped over years by sculptors who attacked the rock out of the stone of their own being, one had Chartres, Notre Dame. Today the stones are made from liquid cooked in vats and rolled into blocks or sheets. Fiberglass, polyethylene, bakelite, styrene, styronware. The environment has less resistance than a river of milk. And the houses and objects built from these liquids are the record of a strifeless war, a liquidation of possibilities. But forgive me for the diatribe.

INTERVIEWER

Then let me give the emphasis here. You say – finally, now, at the end of the day, you remark: form is the record of a war. Of a good war? of a bad war? Of a sharp engagement? or a very dull one? Do I understand you correctly? You are claiming that it is the character of the war which creates the particular style of the form?

MAILER

In all sense of duty I answer: form is the detailed record of an engagement – war reveals the balance of forces, discloses the style of the forces, it hints at the move from potential to the actual.

INTERVIEWER

But what of memory? Does form have no existence in memory?

MAILER

An extraordinary existence in memory. Precisely in

memory. You could even claim that memory like history is nothing but the record of all the oppositions in one's life, of cruel oppositions, calm oppositions, ecstatic oppositions – war, peace, and love, hurrah. Memory is the mind's embodiment of form; therefore, memory, like the mind, is invariably more pure than the event. An event consists not only of forces which are opposed to one another but also of forces which have no relation to the event. Whereas memory has a tendency to retain only the oppositions and the context.

INTERVIEWER

Then can't you say that form is the record of a relationship?

MAILER

Now that I've emphasized its warlike properties, I can agree with you – form is the record of a relationship.

INTERVIEWER

It is that part of the past which is carried into the present? Like memory?

MAILER

It is what survives the relationship. Form is the physical equivalent of memory.

INTERVIEWER

Do you know? This is interesting.

MAILER

(*Gloomy again*) Yes, but it encourages me to go back to our more difficult notions.

INTERVIEWER

Soul? More soul? (*Throws up his hands*) That bloody fucking word. I've heard it too much today. Every time you use it, it leaves an empty space in me.

MAILER

I'm afraid it does. I think the British chose the word so that nobody with blood would ever wish to discuss the subject. They didn't reckon on us poor landless inquirers. Well, we're done. I'm glad it's rounded off.

INTERVIEWER

No, we're not done. You've brought up soul again. What is its direct relation to form? Tell me again.

MAILER

But as I've just explained, it's the father of form. What did you expect it was?

INTERVIEWER

I hoped it would not be the mother.

MAILER

Form is the record of every intent of a soul to express itself upon another soul or spirit, its desire to reveal the shape – which is to say the *mystery* of the time it contains in itself. And it is aided or resisted in achieving that shape by every spirit it encounters. You see we did not begin to discuss a thing. All the problem is still there before us. (*Yawns*) Now, I quit. No more questions.

INTERVIEWER

You have not touched on one huge difficulty. It is false form. For example, I may smile when I am full of hate. Or a girl with small breasts might wear an inflated brassiere, yet you could not tell her breasts are false.

MAILER

Oh, but you could tell – that is what is meant by a fine eye for form.

INTERVIEWER

You cannot always tell.

MAILER

You cannot tell by the shape. But by the mood you can tell, by the presence. That is why form is not shape-by-itself, but shape in the frame of the spirit which contains it.

INTERVIEWER

Oh, now you are perfectly clear.

MAILER

But I am. To myself at any rate. You have pushed me right into the truth. One can distinguish false form from real form by its air, by its presence – do you see? A real form always attracts a spirit which bears a close relation to the war the form was engaged in.

INTERVIEWER

Why? Why should a real form necessarily attract an harmonious spirit?

MAILER

The spirit is not necessarily harmonious so much as truthful. We can detect a real form because it is surrounded by what we perceive subjectively as aesthetic satisfaction, or a sense of elegance, or what we may think of as an air of truth. That air is the spirit which is attached to the real form, and if you ask why a spirit should seek out a form appropriate to it and then manage to muster an air of truth, I tell you it is because spirit can come to rest only in those forms which offer a close relation to the experience of the spirit. Of course, conversely, rest for the spirit offers a glimpse of reality to the soul.

INTERVIEWER

And what does this glimpse of reality for the soul appear to be like?

MAILER

Like the passing sense of grace the alcoholic and the drug addict know. (*Swallows his drink*) And now, friend, I have gotten my mental rocks nicely shifted, and have blown a few minuscule hemorrhages in the upper brain – how we thinkers suffer – and so I will not go on to pursue even one further complication. I am done. I swear to you I am done.

INTERVIEWER

Then can it be you are ready to listen?

MAILER

You have much to offer?

INTERVIEWER

(*Obviously excited by the opportunity*) I've been thinking of what you said at the beginning of the day, about depression and excitation.

MAILER

What did I say?

INTERVIEWER

I think you said excitation applied to a depression creates electricity. Did you have anything in mind?

MAILER

Not that I know of. Of course one always has something in mind.

INTERVIEWER

Well, you know it occurred to me that a magnetic field is like a depression. Everything is pointed in one way. I suppose a magnetic field is the most intense expression of a mood that you could find.

MAILER

Yes, perhaps it is.

INTERVIEWER

So, perhaps, what you meant to say was that while

electricity is created by moving a wire across a magnetic field, in the deeper metaphorical sense it is also created by the purposeful interruption of a mood. Would you care to comment on that?

MAILER

No, I am weary. It is all yours.

INTERVIEWER

I'm beginning to enjoy the Science of Metaphor. I feel ready to explore electricity.

MAILER

Just remember it is a spirit, not a soul. In fact it may even be the spirit of interruption.

INTERVIEWER

I'm pleased to have read your essay on the absurd.

MAILER

Thank you. Cannibals are Christians. And forms which look alike are alike. In some mysterious way. Or at least they are alike until the souls which create them become the spirit of treachery. So says Picasso, I suspect. And in that spirit let me wish you a hearty good night!

A Note of Modest Conclusion

Maybe, it is appropriate to conclude with a piece of prophetic fiction. Assume then that the errors in reasoning and/or judgment you have detected for yourself in these pages are equaled only by the numerous errors you failed to detect. That, scientist and friends, is bound to be the measure of the error in the next prophecy.

The story was written in 1962, therefore was written with the idea of a President not altogether different from John F. Kennedy. L.B.J., needless to say, is altogether different. Go back, if you would go forward in time.

The original prefatory note is also reprinted. It may help to elucidate the style.

THE LAST NIGHT: *A Story*

NOTE TO THE READER: *Obviously a movie must be based on a novel, a story, a play, or an original idea. I suppose it could even derive from a poem. 'Let's do* The Wasteland'*,' said a character of mine named Collie Munshin. The novel may be as much as a thousand pages long, the play a hundred, the story ten, the original idea might be stated in a paragraph. Yet each in its turn must be converted into an art form (a low art form) called a treatment. The treatment usually runs anywhere from twenty to a hundred pages in length. It is a bed of Procrustes. Long stories have their limbs lopped off. Too-brief tales are stretched. The idea is to present for the attention of a producer, a director, or a script reader, in readable but* modest *form, the line of story, the gallery of characters, the pith and gist of your tale.*

But one's duty is to do this without much attempt at style and no attempt at high style. The language must be functional, even cliché, and since one's writing prepares the ground for a movie script, too much introspection in the characters is not encouraged. 'Joey was thinking for the first time that Alice was maybe in love with him' is barely acceptable. An actor on contract could probably manage to register that emotion in a closeup. Whereas,

> *... the little phrase, as soon as it struck his ear, had the power to liberate in him the room that was needed to contain it; the proportions of Swann's soul were altered; a margin was left for a form of enjoyment which corresponded no more than his love for Odette to any external object, and yet was not, like his enjoyment of that love, purely individual, but assumed for him an objective reality superior to that of other concrete things,*

*would bake the clay of a producer's face a little closer to
stone. A producer is interested in the meat and bone of a
story. His question as he reads a treatment is whether he
should go on to assign a writer to do a screenplay of this
story with specific dialogue and most specific situations
added or whether he should ask for another treatment with
new characters and plot, or whether indeed he should write
off the loss and quit right now. So a treatment bears the
same relation to a finished screenplay as the model for a
wind tunnel does to the airplane. Since a treatment is func-
tional, any excellence must be unobtrusive. In fact, a good
director (George Stevens) once told me that good writing in
a treatment was a form of cheating because it introduced
emotional effects through language which he might not as a
director be able to repeat on film.*

*So, thus modestly, I present here a treatment of a movie.
It is based on an original idea. It is a short treatment. Only
a few of the scenes are indicated. As an example of the art
of the treatment, it is not characteristic, for it is written in
somewhat formal prose, but it may have the virtue of
suggesting a motion picture to your imagination.*

*Best wishes. See you in the morning after this last night. –
N.M.*

We're going to describe a movie which will take place
twenty years from now, forty years from now, or is it one
hundred years from now? One cannot locate the date to a
certainty. The world has gone on just about the way we all
expected it would go on. It has had large and dramatic con-
frontations by heads of state, cold wars galore, economic
crises resolved and unresolved, good investment, bad invest-
ment, decent management and a witch's bag full of other
complexities much too numerous ever to bring into a
movie. The result has been a catastrophe which all of us
have dreaded, all of us expected, and none of us has been
able to forestall. The world in twenty or forty years – let us
say it is thirty-six – has come to the point where without an

atomic war, without even a hard or furious shooting war, it has given birth nonetheless to a fearful condition. The world has succeeded in poisoning itself. It is no longer fit to inhabit. The prevalent condition is fallout radiation, anomalous crops, monstrous babies who grow eyes in their navels and die screaming with hatred at the age of six weeks, plastics which emit cancerous fumes, buildings which collapse like camphor flakes, weather which is excruciatingly psychological because it is always too hot or too cold. Governments fall with the regularity of pendulums. The earth is doomed. The number of atom bombs detonated by the Americans, Russians, English, French, the Algerians, Africans, the Israelis and the Chinese, not to mention the Turks, Hindus and Yugoslavians, have so poisoned existence that even the apples on the trees turn malignant in the stomach. Life is being burned out by a bleak fire within, a plague upon the secrets of our existence which stultifies the air. People who govern the nations have come to a modest and simple conclusion. The mistakes of the past have condemned the future. There is no time left to discuss mankind's guilt. No one is innocent of the charge that all have blighted the rose. In fact, the last President to be elected in the United States has come to office precisely by making this the center of his plank: that no one is innocent. The political reactions have been exceptional. Earlier in the century the most fundamental political notion was that guilt could be laid always at the door of one nation and one nation only. Now a man had been elected to one of the two most powerful offices in the world on the premise that the profound illness of mankind was the fault of all, and this victory had prepared the world for cooperative action.

Shortly after the election of this last of the American Presidents, the cold war was finally ended. Russia and America were ready to collaborate, as were Algeria and France, China, England, Western Europe, India and Africa. The fact had finally been faced. Man had succeeded in so polluting the atmosphere that he was doomed to expire himself.

Not one in fifty of the most responsible government scientists would now admit that there were more than twenty years left to life. It was calculated that three quarters of the living population would be gone in five years from the various diseases of fallout. It was further calculated that of the one-quarter remaining women and men, another three-quarters would be dead in the two following years. What a perspective – three-quarters of the people dead in five years, another three-quarters lost in two, one in sixteen left after seven years to watch the slow extinction of the rest. In the face of this fact, led by a President who was exceptional, who was not only the last but perhaps the greatest of America's leaders, the people of the world had come together to stare into the grim alternatives of their fate. All men and women who continued to live on earth would expire. Five hundred thousand at least could survive if they were moved to Mars, perhaps even as many as one million people could be saved, together with various animals, vegetables, minerals and transportable plants. For the rocketeers had made fine advances. Their arts and sciences had developed enormously. They had managed to establish a company of astronauts on Mars. Nearly one thousand had perished earlier on the Moon, but on Mars over a hundred had managed to live; they had succeeded in building a camp out of native vegetation found on the surface. Dwellings had been fabricated from it and, in triumph, a vehicle constructed entirely from materials found on Mars had been sent back to earth, where men and women received it with extravagant hope.

No space here, or for that matter in the movie, to talk of the endless and difficult negotiations which had gone on. The movie could begin perhaps with the ratification of the most astounding piece of legislation ever to be passed in any country. In this case the piece of legislation had been passed by every nation in the world. It was a covenant which declared that every citizen in each nation was going to devote himself to sending a fleet of rocket ships to Mars. This effort would be herculean. It would demand that the heart of each nation's economy be turned over completely to building and equipping ships, selecting the people, training them, and having the moral fortitude to bid them goodbye. In a sense, this universal operation would be equivalent to the evacuation of Dunkirk but with one exception: three-quarters of the British Expeditionary Force was removed safely from the beach. In this case, the world could hope to send up to Mars no more than one million of its people, conceivably less.

It was calculated that the operation must be accomplished in eighteen months – the spread of plague dictated this haste, for half of the remaining members of mankind might be dead in this time and it was felt that to wait too long would be tantamount to populating the ships with human beings too sick, too weak, too plague-ridden to meet the rigors of life on Mars.

It was indeed a heroic piece of legislation, for the people on earth had had the vision to see that all of them were doomed, and so the majority had consented to accept a minority from within themselves to go out further across space and continue the species. Of course, those who were left would make some further effort to build new rocket ships and follow the wave of the first million pioneers, but the chances of this were unlikely. Not only would the resources of the world be used at an unprecedented rate to build a fleet of ten thousand rocket ships capable of carrying one hundred persons each out so far as Mars, but, in fact, as everyone knew, the earth would be stripped of its most exceptional people, its most brilliant technicians, artists, scientists, athletes and executives, plus their families. Those who were left could hardly hope to form a nucleus or a new cadre brilliant enough to repeat the effort. Besides, it was calculated that the ravages of the plague would already be extreme by the time the fleet departed. The heroism of this legislation resided therefore in the fact that man was capable of regarding his fate and determining to do something exceptional about it.

Now the President of the United States, as indicated earlier, was an unusual man. It was a situation right for a dictator, but he was perhaps not only the most brilliant but the most democratic of American Presidents. And one of the reasons the separate nations of the world had been able to agree on this legislation, and the Americans in particular had voted for it, was that the President had succeeded in engaging the imagination of the world's citizens with his project, much as Churchill had brought an incandescence to the morale of the English by the famous speech where he told them he could offer them nothing but blood, sweat, toil and tears. So this President had spared no detail in bringing the citizens of America face to face with the doom of their condition. There were still one hundred million people alive in America. Of that number, one hundred thousand would voyage to Mars. One person in a thousand then could hope to go. Yet there were no riots in the streets. The reason was curious but simple. The President had promised to stay behind and make every effort to train and rally new technicians for the construction of a second fleet. This decision to remain behind had come from many motives: he had recognized the political impossibility of leaving himself – there was moreover sufficient selflessness in the man to make such a course tasteless to him – and, what was also to the point, his wife, whom he loved, was now incurably sick. It had been agreed that the first of the criteria for selection to the fleet was good physical condition, or at least some reasonable suggestion of health, since everyone on earth was now ill in varying degree.

In the first six months after the worldwide ratification of what had already become known as the Legislation For A Fleet, an atmosphere of cooperation, indeed almost of Christian sanctity and good will, came over the earth. Never before in the memory of anyone living had so many people seemed in so good a mood. There was physical suffering everywhere – as has been mentioned, nearly everyone was ill, usually of distressing internal diseases – but the pain now possessed a certain logic, for at least one-half the working force of the world was engaged directly or indirectly in the construction of the Fleet or the preparations surrounding it. Those who were to travel to Mars had a profound sense of mission, of duty and humility. Those who knew they would be left behind felt for the first time in years a sensation of moral weightlessness which was recognized finally as the absence of guilt. Man was at peace with himself. He could even feel hope, because it was, after all, not known to a certainty that those who were left behind must inevitably perish. Some still believed in the possibility of new medical discoveries which could save them. Others devoted themselves to their President's vow that the construction of the second Fleet would begin upon the departure of the first. And, with it all, there was in nearly everyone a sense of personal abnegation, of cooperation, of identification with the community.

It was part of the President's political wisdom that the people who were chosen for the American Fleet had also been selected geographically. Every town of ten thousand inhabitants had ten heroes to make the trip. Not a county of five thousand people scattered over ten thousand square miles of ranches was without its five men, women, and children, all ready. And, of course, for each person chosen there were another ten ready to back them up in case the first man turned ill, or the second, or the third. Behind these ten were one hundred, directly involved in the development, training and morale of each voyager and his ten substitutes. So participation in the flight reached into all the corners of the country, and rare was the family which had nothing to do with it. Historians, writing wistfully about the end of history, had come to the conclusion that man was never so close to finding his soul as in this period when it was generally agreed he was soon to lose his body.

Now, calculate what a blow it was to morality, to courage, and the heart of mankind when it was discovered that life on Mars was not supportable, that the company of a hundred who had been camping on its surface had begun to die, and that their disease was similar to the plague which had begun to visit everyone on earth, but was more virulent in its symptoms and more rapid in its results. The scientific news was overwhelming. Fallout and radiation had poisoned not only the earth but the entire solar system. There was no escape for man to any of the planets. The first solar voyagers to have journeyed so far away as Jupiter had sent back the same tragic news. Belts of radiation incalculably fierce in their intensity now surrounded all the planets.

The President was, of course, the first to receive this news and, in coordination with agreements already arrived at, communicated it to the Premier of the Soviet Union. The two men were already firm friends. They had succeeded, two and a half years before, in forming an alliance to end the Cold War, and by thus acting in concert had encouraged the world to pass the Legislation For A Fleet. Now the Premier informed the President that he had heard the bad news himself: ten of the one hundred men on Mars were, after all, Russians. The two leaders met immediately in Paris for a conference which was brief and critical in its effect. The President was for declaring the news immediately. He had an intimation that to conceal such an apocalyptic fact might invite an unnameable disaster. The Premier of Russia begged him to wait a week at least before announcing this fact. His most cogent argument was that the scientists were entitled to a week to explore the remote possibility of some other solution.

'What other could there possibly be?' asked the President.

'How can I know?' answered the Premier. 'Perhaps we shall find a way to drive a tunnel into the center of the earth in order to burn all impurities out of ourselves.'

The President was adamant. The tragic condition of the world today was precisely the product, he declared, of ten thousand little abuses of power, ten thousand moments in history when the leaders had decided that the news they held was too unpleasant or too paralyzing for the masses to bear.

A new era in history, a heroic if tragic era, had begun precisely because the political leaders of the world now invited the citizens into their confidence. The President and the Premier were at an impasse. The only possible compromise was to wait another twenty-four hours and invite the leaders of Europe, Asia, South America and Africa to an overnight conference which would determine the fate of the news.

The second conference affected the history of everything which was to follow, because all the nations were determined to keep the new and disastrous news a secret. The President's most trusted technical adviser, Anderson Stevens, argued that the general despair would be too great and would paralyze the best efforts of his own men to find another solution. The President and Stevens were old friends. They had come to power together. It was Stevens who had been responsible for some of the most critical scientific discoveries and advances in the rocketry of the last ten years. The Legislation For A Fleet had come, to a great extent, out of his work. He was known as the President's greatest single friend, his most trusted adviser. If he now disagreed with the President at this international conference, the President was obliged to listen to him. Anderson Stevens argued that while the solar system was now poisoned and uninhabitable, it might still be possible to travel to some other part of our galaxy and transfer human life to a more hospitable star. For several days, scientists discussed the possibilities. It was admitted that no fuel or system of booster propulsion was sufficiently powerful to take a rocket ship beyond the solar system. Not even by connecting to booster rockets already in orbit. But then it was also argued that no supreme attempt had yet been made and if the best scientific minds on earth applied themselves to this problem the intellectual results were unforeseeable. In the meantime, absolute silence was to be observed. The program to construct the Martian Fleet was to continue as if nothing had happened. The President acceded to this majority decision of the other leaders, but informed them that he would hold the silence for no more than another week.

By the end of the week, Anderson Stevens returned with an exceptional suggestion: a tunnel ten miles long was to be constructed in all haste in Siberia or the American desert. Pitched at an angle, so that its entrance was on the surface and its base a mile below the earth, the tunnel would act like the muzzle of a rifle and fire the rocket as if it were a shell. Calculated properly, taking advantage of the earth's rotation about its own axis and the greater speed of its rotation about the sun, it was estimated that the rocket ship might then possess sufficient escape velocity to quit the gravitational pull of the sun and so move out to the stars. Since some of the rocket ships were already close to completion and could be adapted quickly to the new scheme, the decision was taken to fire a trial shot in three months, with a picked crew of international experts. If the ship succeeded in escaping the pull of the sun, its crew could then explore out to the nearest stars and send back the essential information necessary for the others who would follow.

Again the question of secrecy was debated. Now Stevens argued that it would be equally irresponsible to give people hope if none would later exist. So, suffering his deepest misgivings, the President consented to a period of silence for three months while the tunnel was completed. In this period, the character of his administration began to change. Hundreds and then thousands of men were keeping two great secrets: the impossibility of life on Mars, and the construction of the giant cannon which would fire an exploratory ship to the stars. So an atmosphere of secrecy and evasion began to circle about the capital, and the mood of the nation was affected. There were rumors everywhere; few of them were accurate. People whispered that the President was dying. Others stated that the Russians were no longer in cooperation with us, but engaged in a contest to see who could get first to Mars. It was said that the climate of Mars had driven the colonists mad, that the spaceships being built would not hold together because the parts were weakened by atomic radiation. It was even rumored – for the existence of the tunnel could not be hidden altogether – that the government was planning to construct an entire state beneath the surface of the earth, in which people could live free of radiation and fallout. For the first time in three or four years, the rates of the sociological diseases – crime, delinquency, divorce and addiction – began again to increase.

The day for the secret test arrived. The rocket was fired. It left the earth's atmosphere at a rate greater than any projectile had yet traveled, a rate so great that the first fear of the scientists was substantiated. The metal out of which the rocket was made, the finest, most heat-resistant alloy yet devised by metallurgists, was still insufficient to withstand the heat of its velocity. As it rose through the air, with the dignitaries of fifty countries gathered to watch its departure, it burst out of the earth, its metal skin glowing with the incandescence of a welding torch, traced a path of incredible velocity across the night sky, so fast that it looked like a bolt of lightning reversed, leaping lively from the earth into the melancholy night, and burned itself out thirty miles up in the air, burned itself out as completely as a dead meteor. No metal existed which could withstand the heat of the excessive friction created by the extreme velocity necessary to blast a ship through the atmosphere and out beyond the gravitational attractions of the sun and its planets. On the other hand, a rocket ship which rose slowly through the earth's atmosphere and so did not overheat could not then generate enough power to overcome the pull of the sun. It seemed now conclusive that man was trapped within his solar system.

The President declared that the people must finally be informed, and in an historic address he did so inform them of the futility of going to Mars and of the impossibility of escape in any other way. There was nothing left for man, he declared, but to prepare himself for his end, to recognize that his soul might have a life beyond his death and so might

communicate the best of himself to the stars. There was thus
the opportunity to die well, in dignity, with grace, and the
hope that the spirit might prove more miraculous and
mighty than the wonders man had extracted from matter. It
was a great speech. Commentators declared it was perhaps
the greatest speech ever delivered by a political leader. It
suffered from one irrevocable flaw: it had been delivered
three months too late. The ultimate reaction was cynical. 'If
all that is left to us is our spirit,' commented a German
newspaper, 'why then did the President deny us three useful
months in which to begin to develop it?'

Like the leaden-green airless evening before an electrical
storm, an atmosphere of depression, bitterness, wildness,
violence and madness rose from the echoes of this speech.
Productivity began to founder. People refused to work.
Teachers taught in classrooms which were empty and left
the schools themselves. Windows began to be broken every-
where, a most minor activity, but it took on accelerated pro-
portions, as if many found a huge satisfaction in throwing
rocks through windows much as though they would pro-
claim that this was what the city would look like when they
were gone. Funerals began to take on a bizarre attraction.
Since ten to twenty times as many people were dying each
day as had died even five years before, funeral processions
took up much of the traffic, and many of the people who
were idle enjoyed marching through the streets in front of
and behind the limousines. The effect was sometimes medi-
eval, for impromptu carnivals began to set themselves up on
the road to the cemetery. There were speeches in Congress
to impeach the President and, as might conventionally be
expected, some of the particular advisers who had counseled
him to keep silence were now most forward in their con-
demnation of his act.

The President himself seemed to be going through an ex-
ceptional experience. That speech in which he had suggested
to mankind that its best hope was to cultivate its spirit
before it died seemed to have had the most profound effect

upon him. His appearance had begun to alter: his hair was subtly longer, his face more gaunt, his eyes feverish. He had always been unorthodox as a President, but now his clothing was often rumpled and he would appear unexpectedly to address meetings or to say a few words on television. His resemblance to Lincoln, which had in the beginning been slight, now became more pronounced. The wits were quick to suggest that he spent hours each day with a makeup expert. In the midst of this, the President's wife died, and in great pain. They had been close for twenty years. Over the last month, he had encouraged her not to take any drugs to dull the pain. The pain was meaningful, he informed her. The choice might be one of suffering now in the present or later in eternity. In anguish she expired. On her deathbed she seared him with a cruel confession. It was that no matter how she had loved him for twenty years, she had always felt there was a part of him never to be trusted, a part which was implacable, inhuman and ruthless. 'You would destroy the world for a principle,' she told him as she died. 'There is something diabolical about you.'

On the return from her funeral, people came out to stand silently in tribute. It was the first spontaneous sign of respect paid to him in some months, and riding alone in the rear of an open limousine, he wept. Yet, before the ride was over, someone in the crowd threw a stone through the windshield. In his mind, as he rode, was the face of his wife, saying to him some months before, 'I tell you, people cannot bear suffering. I know that I cannot. You will force me to destroy a part of your heart if you do not let me have the drugs.'

That night the chief of America's Intelligence Service came to see the President. The Russians were engaged in a curious act. They were building a tunnel in Siberia, a tunnel even larger than the American one, and at an impossible angle; it went almost directly into the earth and then took a jog at right angles to itself. The President put through a call to Moscow to speak to the Premier. The Premier told the President that he had already made preparations to see him.

There was a matter of the most extreme importance to be discussed: the Russians had found a way to get a rocket ship out of the solar system.

So, the two men met in London in a secret conference. Alone in a room, the Premier explained the new project and his peculiar position. Slowly, insidiously he had been losing control in his country, just as the President had become progressively more powerless in America. Against the Premier's wishes, some atomic and rocket scientists had come together on a fearsome scheme which the Army was now supporting. It had been calculated that if an ordinary rocket ship, of the sort which belonged to the Martian Fleet, were fired out from the earth, it would be possible to blast it into the furthest reaches of our own galaxy, provided – and this was most important – a planet were exploded at the proper moment. It would be like the impetus a breaking wave could give to a surfboard rider. With proper timing the force released by blowing up the planet would more than counteract the gravitational pull of the sun. Moreover, the rocket ship could be a great distance away from the planet at the moment it was exploded, and so the metal of its skin would not have to undergo any excessive heat.

'But which planet could we use?' asked the President.

The two men looked at one another. The communication passed silently from one's mind to the other. It was obvious. With the techniques available to them there was only one planet: the earth.

That was what the Russian tunnel was for. A tunnel going deep into the earth, loaded with fissionable material, and exploded by a radio wave sent out from a rocket ship already one million miles away. The detonation of the earth would hurl the rocket ship like a pebble across a chasm of space.

'Well,' says the President, after a long pause, 'it may be possible for the Fleet to take a trip after all.'

'No,' the Premier assures him, 'not the Fleet.' For the earth would be detonated by an atomic chain reaction which would spew radioactive material across one hundred million miles of the heavens. The alloy vuranel was the only alloy which could protect a rocket ship against the electronic hurricane which would follow the explosion. There was on earth enough vuranel to create a satisfactory shield for only one ship. 'Not a million men, women, and children, but a hundred, a hundred people and a few animals will take the trip to a star.'

'Who will go?' asks the President.

'Some of your people,' answers the Premier, 'some of mine. You and me.'

'I won't go,' says the President.

'Of course you will,' says the Premier. 'Because if you don't go, I don't go, and we've been through too much already. You see, my dear friend, you're the only equal I have on earth. It would be much too depressing to move through those idiotic stars without you.'

But the President is overcome by the proportions of the adventure. 'You mean we will blow up the entire world in order that a hundred people have some small chance – one chance in five, one chance in ten, one chance in a hundred, or less – to reach some star and live upon it. The odds are too brutal. The cost is incalculable.'

'We lose nothing but a few years,' says the Premier. 'We'll all be dead anyway.'

'No,' says the President, 'it's not the same. We don't know what we destroy. It may be that after life ceases on the earth, life will generate itself again, if only we leave the earth alone. To destroy it is monstrous. We may destroy the spirit of something far larger than ourselves.'

The Premier taps him on the shoulder. 'Look, my friend, do you believe that God is found in a cockroach? I don't. God is found inside you, and inside me. When all of us are gone, God is also gone.'

'I don't know if I believe that,' answers the President.

Well, the Premier tells him, religious discussion has always fascinated him, but politics are more pressing. The question is whether they are at liberty to discuss this matter on its moral merits alone. The tunnel in Siberia had been built without his permission. It might interest the President to know that a tunnel equally secret is being constructed near the site of the old Arizona tunnel. There were Russian technicians working on that, just as American technicians had been working in Siberia. The sad political fact is that the technicians had acquired enormous political force, and if it were a question of a showdown tomorrow, it is quite likely they could seize power in the Soviet Union and in America as well.

'You, sir,' says the Premier, 'have been searching your soul for the last year in order to discover reasons for still governing. I have been studying Machiavelli because I have found, to my amusement, that when all else is gone, when life is gone, when the promise of future life is gone, and the meaning of power, then what remains for one is the game. I want the game to go on. I do not want to lose power in my country. I do not want you to lose it in yours. I want, if necessary, to take the game clear up into the stars. You deserve to be on that rocket ship, and I deserve to be on it. It is possible we have given as much as anyone alive to brooding over the problems of mankind in these last few years. It is your right and my right to look for a continuation of the species. Perhaps it is even our duty.'

'No,' says the President. 'They're holding a gun to our heads. One cannot speak of the pleasures of the game or of honor or of duty when there is no choice.'

He will not consent to destroying the earth unless the people of earth choose that course, with a full knowledge of the consequences. What is he going to do, asks the Premier. He is going to tell the world, says the President. There must be a general worldwide election to determine the decision.

'Your own people will arrest you first,' says the Premier. He then discloses that the concept of exploding the earth to boost the power of the rocket had been Anderson Stevens' idea.

The President picks up the phone and makes a call to his press chief. He tells him to prepare the television networks for an address he will deliver that night. The press chief asks him the subject. The President tells him he will discuss it upon his return. The press chief says that the networks cannot be cleared unless the President informs him now of the subject. It will be a religious address, says the President.

'The networks may not give us the time,' says the press chief. 'Frankly, sir, they are not certain which audiences share your spiritual fire.'

The President hangs up. 'You are right,' he tells the Premier. 'They will not let me make the speech. I have to make it here in London. Will you stand beside me?'

'No, my friend,' says the Russian, 'I will not. They will put you in jail for making that speech, and you will have need of me on the outside to liberate your skin.'

The President makes the address in London to the citizens of the world. He explains the alternatives, outlines his doubts, discusses the fact that there are technicians ready to seize power, determined to commit themselves to the terrestrial explosion. No one but the people of the earth, by democratic procedure, have the right to make this decision, he declares, and recommends that as a first step the people march on the tunnel sites and hold them. He concludes his address by saying he is flying immediately back to Washington and will be there within two hours.

The message has been delivered on the network devoted to international television. It reaches a modest percentage of all listeners in the world. But in America, from the President's point of view the program took place at an unfortunate time, for it was the early hours of the morning. When he lands in Washington at dawn, he is met by his Cabinet and a platoon of M.P.s, who arrest him. Television in America is devoted that morning to the announcement that the President has had a psychotic breakdown and is at present under observation by psychiatrists.

For a week, the atmosphere is unendurable. A small percentage of the people in America have listened to the President's speech. Many more have heard him in other countries. Political tensions are acute, and increase when the Premier of the Soviet Union announces in reply to a question from a reporter that in his opinion the President of the United States is perfectly sane. Committees of citizens form everywhere to demand an open investigation of the charges against the President. It becomes a rallying cry that the President be shown to the public. A condition close to civil war exists in America.

At this point, the President is paid a visit by Anderson Stevens, the scientist in charge of the rocket program, the man who has lately done more than any other to lead the Cabinet against the President. Now they have a conversation behind the barred windows of the hospital room where the President is imprisoned. Anderson Stevens tells the President that the first tunnel which had been built for the star shot was, from his point of view, a ruse. He had never expected that rocket ship, which was fired like a bullet, to escape from the earth's atmosphere without burning to a cinder. All of his experience had told him it would be destroyed. But he had advanced the program for that shot because he wished to test something else – the tunnel. It had been essential to discover how deeply one could dig into the crust of the earth before the heat became insupportable for an atomic bomb. In effect, the tunnel had been dug as a test to determine the feasibility of detonating the earth. And so that shot which had burned up a rocket ship had been, from Stevens' point of view, a success, because he had learned that the tunnel could be dug deep enough to enable a superior hydrogen bomb to set off a chain reaction in the fiery core of the earth. The fact that one hundred rocketeers and astronauts, men who had been his friends for decades, had died in an experiment he had known to be all but hopeless was an indication of how serious he was about the earth bomb shot. The President must not think for a moment that Stevens would hesitate to keep him in captivity, man the ship himself, and blow up the earth.

Why, then, asks the President, does Stevens bother to speak to him? Because, answers Stevens, he wants the President to command the ship. Why? Because in some way the fate of the ship might be affected by the emotions of everybody on earth at the moment the earth was exploded. This sounded like madness to some of his scientific colleagues, but to him it was feasible that if life had a spirit and all life ceased to exist at the same moment, then that spirit, at the instant of death, might have a force of liberation or deterrence which could be felt as a physical force across the heavens.

'You mean,' says the President, 'that even in the ruthless circuits of your heart there is terror, a moral terror, at the consequence of your act. And it is me you wish to bear the moral consequence of that act, and not you.'

'You are the only man great enough, sir,' says Anderson Stevens, bowing his head.

'But I think the act is wrong,' says the President.

'I know it is right,' says Stevens. 'I spent a thousand days and a thousand nights living with the terror that I might be wrong, and still I believe I am right. There is something in me which knows that two things are true – that we have destroyed this earth not only because we were not worthy of it, but because it may have been too cruel for us. I tell you, we do not know. Man may have been mismated with earth. In some fantastic way, perhaps we voyaged here some millions of years ago and fell into a stupidity equal to the apes. That I don't know. But I do know, if I know anything at all, because my mind imprisoned in each and every one of my cells tells me so, that we must go on, that we as men are different from the earth, we are visitors upon it. We cannot suffer ourselves to sit here and be extinguished, not when the beauty which first gave speech to our tongues commands us to go out and find another world, another earth, where we may strive, where we may win, where we may find the right to live again. For that dream I would kill everyone on earth.

I would kill my children. In fact I must, for they will not accompany me on the trip. And you,' he says to the President, 'you must accompany us. You must help to make this trip. For we as men may finally achieve greatness if we survive this, the most profound of our perils.'

'I do not trust myself,' says the President. 'I do not know if my motive is good. Too many men go to their death with a hatred deep beyond words, wishing with their last breath that they could find the power to destroy God. I do not know – I may be one of those men.'

'You have no choice,' says Anderson Stevens. 'There are people trying to liberate you now. I shall be here to shoot you myself before they succeed. Unless you agree to command the ship.'

'Why should I agree?' says the President. 'Shoot me now.'

'No,' says Stevens, 'you will agree, because I will make one critical concession to you. I do it not from choice, but from desperation. My dreams tell me we are doomed unless you command us. So I will let you give the people their one last opportunity. I will let you speak to them. I will put my power behind you, so that they may vote.'

'No,' says the President, 'not yet. Because if such an election were lost, if the people said, "Let us stay here and die together, and leave the earth to mend itself, without the sound of human speech or our machines," then you would betray me. I know it. You would betray everyone. Some night, in some desert, a rocket ship would be fired up into the sky, and twenty hours later, deep in some secret tunnel, all of us would be awakened by the last explosion of them all. No. I will wait for the people to free me first. Of necessity, my first act then will be to imprison you.'

After this interview between Stevens and the President, the ruling coalition of Cabinet officers and technicians refused, of course, to let the people see the President. The response was a virtually spontaneous trek of Americans by airplane, helicopter, automobile, by animal, by motorcycle, and on foot, toward the tunnel site the President had named.

The Army was quickly deployed to prevent them, but the soldiers refused to protect the approaches to the tunnel. They also asked for the right to see the President. The Cabinet capitulated. The President was presented on television. He announced that the only justification for the star ship was a worldwide general election.

The most brilliant, anguished, closely debated election in the history of the world now took place. For two months, argument licked like flame at the problem. In a last crucial speech the night before the election, the President declared that it was the words of a man now in prison, Anderson Stevens, which convinced him how he would vote. For he, the President, had indeed come to believe that man rising out of the fiery grave of earth, out of the loss of his past, his history, and his roots, might finally achieve the greatness and the goodness expected of him precisely because he had survived this, the last and the most excruciating of his trials. 'If even a few of us manage to live, our seed will be changed forever by the self-sacrifice and nobility, the courage and the loss engraved on our memory of that earth-doomed man who was our ancestor and who offered us life. Man may become human at last.' The President concluded his speech by announcing that if the people considered him deserving the honor, he would be the first to enter the ship, he would take upon himself the act of pressing that button which would blow up the earth.

The answer to this speech was a solemn vote taken in favor of destroying the world, and giving the spaceship its opportunity to reach the stars.

The beginning of the last sequence in the movie might show the President and the Premier saying goodbye. The Premier has discovered he is now hopelessly ill, and so will stay behind.

The Premier smiles as he says goodbye. 'You see, I am really too fat for a brand-new game. It is you fanatics who always take the longest trips.'

One hundred men and women file into the ship behind the

President. The rocket is fired and rises slowly, monumentally. Soon it is out of sight. In the navigation tower within the rocket the President stares back at earth. It is seen on a color television screen, magnified enormously. The hours go by and the time is approaching for the explosion. The radio which will send out the wave of detonation is warmed up. Over it the President speaks to the people who are left behind on earth. All work has of course ceased, and people waiting through the last few hours collect, many of them, in public places, listening to the President's voice on loudspeakers. Others hear it on radios in their rooms, or sprawled on the grass in city parks. People listen in cars on country crossroads, at the beach, watching the surf break. Quietly, a few still buy tickets for their children on the pony rides. One or two old scholars sit by themselves at desks in the public library, reading books. Some drink in bars. Others sit quietly on the edge of pavements, their feet in the street. One man takes his shoes off. The mood is not too different from the mood of a big city late at night when the weather is warm. There is the same air of expectation, of quiet, brooding concentration.

'Pray for us,' says the President to them, speaking into his microphone on that rocket ship one million miles away. 'Pray for us. Pray that our purpose is good and not evil. Pray that we are true and not false. Pray that it is part of our mission to bring the life we know to other stars.' And in his ears he hears the voice of his wife, saying through her pain, 'You will end up by destroying everything.'

'Forgive me, all of you,' says the President. 'May I be an honest man and not first deluded physician to the Devil.' Then he presses the button.

The earth detonates into the dark spaces. A flame leaps across the solar system. A scream of anguish, jubilation, desperation, terror, ecstasy, vaults across the heavens. The tortured heart of the earth has finally found its voice. We have a glimpse of the spaceship, a silver mirror of light, streaming into the oceans of mystery, and the darkness beyond.

IN THE JARDIN EXOTIQUE OF EZE

In the Jardin Exotique of Eze
the cactus come up from the sea
like an anemone wooing a spider
or a pygmy with a blowgun dart.
Silently they smell the breeze,
        invertebrate,
their memory as long as the tripe of the Mediterranée.
Was it once or never? that a God from deep waters
                    dreaming of the moon
fell in love with a gleam from the midnight sky
who, intoxicated with herself
and the rapture of the depths,
like a daughter most fortunate in family,
beautiful, spoiled, innocent of alarm,
wandered down an alley
dark as the pitch of blackest frustration
and there was trapped by the sound of need
in the murmur of an ape.
So did that God of dark waters woo a moon beam
and from their love leave a seed
on the spume of the wrack
which washes a desert shore.
Cactus,
mad psychotic bulb of light and dark
        spy of the deep sea
        intimate of the moon
your form inspires nausea
for love which dares too much
and has no soil but sand
flowers spines of lunar hatred
shapes tubers on the leaf
and gives no wine but visions from peyote

of ether and her gardens
which burn in gloom
of poison, bliss, the death of suns
and phosphorescent nights.

THE WORLD'S GREATEST NOVELISTS
NOW AVAILABLE IN PANTHER BOOKS

John O'Hara

Ourselves to Know	£1.50 ☐
Ten North Frederick	£1.50 ☐
A Rage to Live	60p ☐

Norman Mailer

The Fight (Non-Fiction)	75p ☐
The Presidential Papers	95p ☐
Barbary Shore	40p ☐
Advertisements for Myself	50p ☐
An American Dream	£1.25 ☐
The Naked and The Dead	£1.50 ☐

Kingsley Amis

Ending Up	60p ☐
The Riverside Villas Murder	95p ☐
I Like It Here	50p ☐
That Uncertain Feeling	50p ☐
Girl 20	40p ☐
I Want It Now	60p ☐
The Green Man	95p ☐

Kurt Vonnegut Jr

Wampeters, Foma & Granfalloons	95p ☐
Between Time and Timbuktu	£1.50 ☐
Breakfast of Champions	95p ☐
Mother Night	60p ☐
Slaughterhouse 5	75p ☐
Player Piano	95p ☐
Welcome to the Monkey House	95p ☐
God Bless You, Mr Rosewater	95p ☐

THE WORLD'S GREATEST NOVELISTS
NOW AVAILABLE IN PANTHER BOOKS

Simon Raven

Bring Forth The Body	90p
The Survivors	95p
Come Like Shadows	65p
Sound the Retreat	50p
The Feathers of Death	35p
Friends in Low Places	35p
Fielding Gray	30p
Doctors Wear Scarlet	30p

Paul Scott

The Raj Quartet

The Towers of Silence	£1.25	☐
The Day of the Scorpion	£1.25	☐
The Jewel in the Crown	£1.25	☐
A Division of the Spoils	£1.50	☐
The Bender	75p	☐
The Corrida at San Feliu	75p	☐
A Male Child	50p	☐
The Alien Sky	50p	☐
The Chinese Love Pavilion	50p	☐

All these books are available at your local bookshop or newsagent, or can be ordered direct from the publisher. Just tick the titles you want and fill in the form below.

Name..

Address...

....

Write to Panther Cash Sales, PO Box 11, Falmouth, Cornwall TR10 9EN.
Please enclose remittance to the value of the cover price plus:

UK: 22p for the first book plus 10p per copy for each additional book ordered to a maximum charge of 82p.

BFPO and EIRE: 22p for the first book plus 10p per copy for the next 6 books, thereafter 3p per book.

OVERSEAS: 30p for the first book and 10p for each additional book.
Granada Publishing reserve the right to show new retail prices on covers, which may differ from those previously advertised in the text or elsewhere.